ROAD TRIP TO FREEDOM

ROBIN DIVINE

Also by Robin Divine

Choose Happiness: 100 Short, Sweet Life Reminders

Copyright © 2016 by Robin Divine

All rights reserved. No part of this publication may be reproduced, distributed, or transmitted in any form or by any means, including photocopying, recording, or other electronic or mechanical methods, without the prior written permission of the publisher, except in the case of brief quotations embodied in critical reviews and certain other noncommercial uses permitted by copyright law.

KiMani, my journey brought me to you and my heart has always known your name. Through the many paths we have traveled to find one another, I have loved you. You are my best friend, my safe place and you have my heart. You saw me when no else did. You acknowledged my light when I didn't even know that I had any. Thank you for standing with me, for me and beside me. I love you to the moon and back.

Amy and Pamela, I could not have asked for kinder people to begin and end my journey with, love you both.

Aurora, Joli, Victoria, Rachel, Teena and Amy C.M., thank you for being the most joyful and creative soul sisters a traveling gal could ask for. You brightened up many of my darkest days with your light.

Jo and Jane, you two are the best Road Trip Mama's around. Thank you.

To the most rockstar editor out there, I thank you Donniee Barnes.

Tunez and Niall, I am beyond grateful for your creativity and patience in this process.

To my fellow travelers, we did it. Thank you for holding my hand.

To the Road Trip!

SENTIMENTS ABOUT THE ROAD TRIP

*

This is the story of my Road Trip. Robin's Road Trip to Freedom.

However, before I start, I wanted to share a handful of the comments that I've received about the trip. I intended to condense it to one page but that didn't seem sufficient for the amount of unconditioned love, support and genuine kindness that had been shown to me during the journey. Instead, I dedicate the next two pages to sharing that love with you.

I will say that through your adventure, I have seen that there is a large amount of compassion and kindness out there. Your trip has provided a stark contrast to other events that have been going on. Your life is a blessing to somebody. ~Anthony

Thank you for raising our collective energy with your genuine positive loving attitude. ~Ka

You have such a special place in my heart. Thank you for sharing your journey with us, thank you for being you. ~Charlena

You give me hope to continue to step into the unknown on faith. ~Deborah

Because you opened yourself up to feel and trusted us enough to share those feelings, we have all come together to hold space for each others' healing. ~Jessica

You should be proud of taking the leap of faith that many of us would be too terrified to take. ~Jo

We are on different journeys right now, but you wouldn't believe how much of what you said is exactly what I needed to hear! ~Teena

You inspire others because of how down-to-earth you are and how people relate to you. You're willing to discuss trials, difficulties, doubts, and even a crisis of faith. You have such a good heart. We see your genuineness and leaving all expectations at the door, support you wholeheartedly and wish you love and light. ~Erika

You are laying a path for others to follow whether it is on a road trip, backpacking through Europe or any other journey. You are doing it fearlessly and we are with you every step of the way. ~Donna

My dear, with your candid lines, you directly touch our hearts. You reach out for us. You speak out our darkest moments which we don't have the courage to even confess. ~Nadja

I appreciate your organic honesty, your unguarded humanness. ~Victoria

Sista, you share souldippin' words to reach global understanding. Thank you for that. ~Anette

The thing that makes your stories so heartwarming and interesting is that you are real. You don't always have the answers and you don't always know what to do. And sometimes you feel miserable and you tell us about it, yet you keep on keepin' on. I love you for that! ~Elizabeth

You are the bravest boldest motha' I know right about now. I know what Robin who hides and operates from fear looks like. Who you are now is a woman who has grown so far beyond that. Your embracing of your experience with embarking on this road trip was and continues to be a move that turns all established, traditional, mass consciousness notions on their head. You stopped fighting to do the "norm" and you also didn't succumb to despair. You carved out a path, not knowing where it would lead. However, we know that all roads lead to home, and your soul knew where you needed to go. You continue to be an inspiration. ~Kimberly

Thank you for having the balls to share your heart. ~Debra

To me, that last one was the best comment ever in life. Thank you, everyone. Your words made more of a difference than you will ever know.

*

*

Where would you have me go?
What would you have me do?
What would you have me say and to whom?

~Marianne Williamson

*

The following writings are the story of my cross country journey. I began my travels in Virginia on May 17, 2012 and brought the trip to a close on February 10, 2013 in New Jersey. Over the course of nine months and over 50,000 miles, I made my way to the sunny Pacific California Highway coast and then back to the icy East coast. I didn't intend for it to be a spiritual trip and yet that was how it unfolded. In May 2012, I found myself without a home and with little money to my name. And by "little" I mean twenty dollars. Years of unloving choices had brought me to that point. The details of those choices are not important at the moment. What is important is that I had found myself in that situation.

After the shame of being asked to leave the home of a relative where I had overstayed my welcome (by many moons) and the fear of not knowing what was next subsided, I made the choice to respond from a place of surrender. How did I get to surrender? It took a minute. While talking to a friend about what in the fresh hell I was going to do with the pile of craptasticness that I had created in my life, she suggested that I approach this by making an empowered choice as opposed to one that felt completely powerless. The outcome of that was Robin's Road Trip to Freedom.

I would soon head out on the road to a journey with no set destination. I had no idea that it would change my life. I traveled with two suitcases full of clothes, a handful of sentimental items, a pillow and a blanket. The rest of my possessions were placed in a small storage unit. In my pocket was my last $20. What made the situation feel even more like a cosmic joke was that I did not have a cell phone or a computer to travel with. The means by which I was able to traverse from coast to coast were incomparable human kindness, unrelenting faith and *complete* trust of the Universe.

From May 2012 to February 2013, I traveled over 75,000 miles. I stayed in a hotel only once (a gift from a fellow traveler) and the rest of the time was spent with people that opened their homes and their hearts to me along the way. A handful were friends; the rest were "strangers" that only knew that I was in need. This is how I know it was a spiritual journey. Who else but Spirit/Source (which ever name you choose to call it) could open people's hearts and their doors the way that they were opened to me? As I look back, it is astounding to me the state of guidance, protection and grace that I traveled under.

I abandoned my daily journal entries often and my photos are minimal. However, the story is still told. The following writings are from a Facebook page that I created called Robin's Road Trip to Freedom. I wanted people to be able to travel along side me; I also needed the companionship. During those 9 months, not only did I renew my spirit for life but I also found love. Love for myself as well as love for others.

I didn't come out of this experience knowing all the answers and I didn't do it all the "right" way. I'm not special in my story. I just wanted life to be better and I didn't allow anything or anyone to allow me to believe that was not possible. I followed my heart and I *didn't ever give up* even though I wanted to over and over again. It is my hope that this journey inspires you to live your life always expecting goodness regardless of where you have been.

During my Road Trip to Freedom, over 1,500 fellow travelers virtually joined me on the road. Many of those that followed, supported and loved me through this journey came from an earlier Facebook page that I had created in 2011 called "Choose Happiness." Over the course of a few years, Choose Happiness grew into our own tight knit tribe of over 100,000 people that simply wanted to remind each other to stay encouraged and live happy.

To keep my own self encouraged as I traveled, I wrote. Below is a journal entry that genuinely represents the heart of the trip for me:

December 15, 2012 (Guadalupe, CA)

This journey has been one "show me what you got" moment after another. It's not from a harsh place. It's more the Universe gently saying "I see you. I know your strength. I know what you're capable of." Show me what you got.

Robin, when life breaks your heart and takes away the things you thought you could not live without, show me what you got.

When you find yourself in uncertain situations and it takes every bit of your being to trust in the Universe, show me what you got.

That moment in which your deepest fears are in your face and you can't hide, show me what you got.

And then yesterday, I heard it again.

"Beloved, in the midst of all that is, show me what you got."

Thank you for sharing in my journey and joining me as I *"show you what I got."*

To the Road Trip!

~Robin

The following posts are in date order. I have updated the entries to include current thoughts and unshared details. It has taken me over two years to fully wrap my heart and my head around all that I experienced. I'm now ready to share those parts of the journey which I had kept hidden away, even from myself.

Recent reflections are written in *italics*. You can read the journey in the order that it unfolded or choose a day and find the pieces of the entry that resonate with you. Whichever way you read it is just right. Make this journey your own.

> *"Because she could, she did. And when she was told she could not, she simply did not listen."*
>
> *~ Chey Davis (my friend and a fellow traveler)*

Utter terror, confusion and upset. That's what I was feeling as I sat down to write this first post. I felt as though I had nothing. I had this intense knowing that how I responded to this situation would have a fundamental impact on the rest of my life. I was at a choice point. This was either going to take me out or support me in building a completely new foundation for myself. I had to decide with care. I had to be vigilant with every thought that crossed my mind. I had to hold onto hope at all costs and see the good regardless of how challenging it was. My words were sincere. With that said, it often took everything in me to reach for a higher thought as I wrote. I had to.

April 23, 2012 (Suffolk, VA)

Yo! It's time to Road Trip! You will *never* guess what I won. I won a trip across the country and around the world! Ok, I didn't win it. I was asked to leave my current living space and I have nowhere to go. Close enough, right? And when I say "nowhere" I actually mean everywhere!

Here's the interesting part: my car is in the shop, my pockets are lined with gum wrappers and I am sans laptop, cell phone and other technology. Challenge accepted!

What did you say, have I lost it? A little bit, yeah. But if you really knew how low I was right now, then you would understand that I have no choice but to go up from here.

To that I say, let the manifestations of goodness, JOY and adventure begin!

16 days until I hit the road. C'mon and join me. I have a seat just for you. I'm a bit nervous so I could use the company.

Curious about how this is going to unfold? So am I. Road Trip 2012, let's do this.

Official start date: May 17, 2012.

-Robin

*Why May 17th? A fair question. The relatives I was staying with were going on vacation...and they wanted me out by the time they got back. I found this out

indirectly from their handyman during a casual conversation as I helped him pull weeds from the lawn. It went like this:

Him: So, did you know they're going to Hawaii in a few weeks?
Me: Yep…
Him: Did you know they want you gone when they get back?
Me: Hmmm, nope. Damn. Good to know…

Alrighty then. May 17th it is. I had three weeks to figure out where my life was headed next and how I was going to get there.

April 24, 2012 (Suffolk, VA)

Reality is overrated. That's it.

~Robin

*I kept asking myself "is this real life?" Nothing about my life at that point felt real to me. "How do I have nothing? How do I have no where to go? How do I not have anyone to call?" I could not comprehend that this was the "reality" that I had created.

April 25, 2012 (Suffolk, VA)

"Adventure begins when comfort has left you." ~Anonymous

Comfort has left, I'm open to the adventure.

~Robin

April 26, 2012 (Suffolk, VA)

I don't think that I'm thinking clearly but I can't tell. More than likely I'm not. I'm ok with that.

~Robin

*I was starting to unravel and I knew it. Not only did I know it, I was alright with it. I had even started to believe that this trip was potentially a "sane" idea. Let's just say that my mind was working overtime in an attempt to make the situation less painful for me.

April 29, 2012 (Suffolk, VA)

Have you ever wanted to hop on a plane or get in the car and just leave on a Road Trip? What made you go for it or how come you waited? Would you do it again? I'm full of questions. What can I say, I'm curious. Come share some of your experiences, I'd love to hear about your adventures.

~Robin

I was desperate for someone to say "no, you're not ridiculous for doing this." You're going to be ok. I never heard anyone say it. So instead, I kept saying it to myself. Every day. I said it over and over again until I started to believe it.

April 30, 2012 (Suffolk, VA)

Random thought for the day: Put your plans away every now and then and let the unknown carry you.

~Robin

May 1, 2012 (Suffolk, VA)

I need to go somewhere quiet.
I need a place to call home.
Oh hell, I don't know what I need...

~Robin

There were days where all I wanted to do was crawl into bed and pretend that my current situation wasn't happening. The repetitive thought of "you're not going to have a bed in two weeks" was the main reason I kept moving forward.

May 2, 2012 (Suffolk, VA)

Any fellow travelers out there with me yet? Am I really going on a Road Trip? I suppose we'll find out together. Hey, I like that. Fellow travelers. Makes me feel as if I'm not quite so alone in this.

Road Trip start date: May 17, 2012. 15 days to go.

~Robin

May 3, 2012 (Suffolk, VA)

"Faith is not being sure where you are going and going anyway."
~Frederick Buechner

Last night I went to bed with a calm and quiet confidence. This morning I awoke with an overwhelming sense of fear and doubt. I believe that you shouldn't tell everyone everything. There are some events that should be cherished and kept sacred. This journey is sacred to me. I share it with you all because I feel a genuine sense of love and support in your words. I have so much gratitude to you for that.

Yesterday an acquaintance questioned me about where I was headed and what the "plan" was. My response was: "I'm leaving." There was no more that needed to be said. The next hour of our car ride went like this:

"You're just leaving? With *no* plan? With *no* money? That is such a *terrible* idea. *Anything* could happen! You could run out of gas or break down and get stranded, then what?! People are *really bad* out there. I know it would make you unhappy but why don't you do (insert random opinion) instead? Doesn't that *sound* better? What you are doing will *never* work!"

I opened my mind to hear the words and closed my heart to protect it from the harshness. Had I not, I may never have had the courage to move forward. As I continued to listen I silently began to affirm the Truth in my mind:

"You are so loved. You are supported. Your every need will be provided for. No one has to understand it, go find what you are in search of. People are good, kind and caring. These are the people that will nurture you along the way. Have Faith in yourself. Trust the process. You are not alone. Enjoy the journey."

I pray that I am right as I repeat the words over and over.

"You are so loved."

I repeat it again until it becomes my mantra. I repeat it until it begins to feel real.

"Trust the process."

I call to mind every "self help" book and spiritual class that I have taken to help me gather the courage to quell the noise that says they might be right.

"You are not alone."

I continued to affirm encouragement throughout the night. However, the next day I awoke to a suffocating feeling of fear. Fear? Fear?! There's no fear on Robin's Road Trip to Freedom! Today there is, and that's ok. The issue isn't the fear. The issue is: How do I respond in the face of it? Do I allow it to immobilize me and abandon what I know to be True? Or do I continue to take steps forward even if they are unsteady? I acknowledge my fear but I choose not to feed it. I choose to remember the Truth instead.

Road Trip to Freedom 2012, here I come. I can do this! I can do this.

Road Trip start date: May 17, 2012. 14 days to go.

~Robin

Looking back on that experience, what I learned was this: people are always going to have their opinions of my life and how I should or shouldn't live it. In response to these people, I now say "thanks for sharing" and then I keep on doing me. I may stumble along the way with missteps and that's okay, at least they'll be mine.

May 5, 2012 (Suffolk, VA)

My mantra for the day: The Universe is my nest. I am always supported. I have all that I need.

Road Trip start date May 17th, 2012: 12 days to go.

~Robin

As a lifetime (wayward) student of Metaphysics, I knew that the Universe was abundant. Remembering to keep that in the forefront of my mind was a daily exercise in perseverance.

May 6, 2012 (Suffolk, VA)

Robin's random upcoming travel tip for the day: Trust your instincts. Stay present. Be mindful.

On a side note: that can apply to Road Trips and life.

Road Trip start date May 17th, 2012: 11 days to go.

~Robin

May 6, 2012 (Suffolk, VA)

I just tossed out some clothes from my bag to make more space for books. At the top to the reading list: "The Big Leap" by Gay Hendricks. That seems like appropriate reading for the trip ahead.

~Robin

The Big Leap is about just that: taking big leaps in life. Like I said, the book was quite fitting.

May 7, 2012 (Suffolk, VA)

This day has kicked my behind in all kinds of creative ways and I'm still here. I did it. The journey that I thought would never end is coming to a close. I am grateful.

~Robin

That was my last day in the space that had felt like a prison to me from the moment I arrived. The time that I spent there was the most emotionally stuck that I had ever been in my life. I felt relegated to my one room (my own doing) and my eating habits were confined to whatever I could microwave or fit in my toaster oven. I knew that I needed to be anywhere but there but I had no idea how to free my mind and myself. This was a way out. As uncertain and intimidating as the future felt, there was also a sense of incomparable relief that came with knowing that chapter of my story was complete.

May 8, 2012 (Suffolk, VA)

I can't believe it's almost time for the Road Trip. But first, I'm headed out for a short mental health break before I get on the road. I leave for the airport in a couple of hours. The only thing is, my flight doesn't leave until 7am…tomorrow. 21 hours in an airport? Could be a good time. If not, then I'll do my damnedest to make it one. Are you ready to Road Trip? I very possibly maybe might just be. Check with me in the morning. See you on the 17th! Thanks for the support everyone.

~Robin

*Thanks to a long time college friend, I spent the days of May 9-16th in California. He, sensing my stress level at the upcoming journey, gifted me a ticket there to visit with him and rest before my Road Trip.

May 13, 2012 (Los Angeles, CA)

Good morning everyone! What a trip it's been so far. A handful of highs, a few interesting firsts and a couple of unexpected lows. But overall, it's been incredible. I needed this. My emotions have been so up and down in the past week but I suppose that is to be expected. On one hand, I'm excited to embark on the adventure of a Road Trip! On the other hand, all I want to do is go home, rest and lead a quiet life. My hope is that at the end of this trip, I'll be able to create that for myself: a comforting home that welcomes me back after my travels.

I'm still in California for a few days and today we head to Hollywood. The vegan goodness here has been incredible and I've fallen in love with Native Foods Cafe. My goal is to try everything on the menu before I leave. I have faith in my eating abilities.

And finally, a Happy Mother's Day to all the Moms out there! Thank you for nurturing, guiding and supporting us on this ultimate "wait, what in the hell?!" adventure called Life. Even when we don't always know where we are going, you're there.

Have a beautiful day everyone, see you soon!

~Robin

*It was days like these that I wished I would have written in my journal more. What were the highs, the lows and the firsts? C'mon Robin, I need details! As for a high, I do remember that I had the opportunity have lunch with a fellow traveler and friend that I had met on my Choose Happiness page when I first started it in 2011. I named her "Mama Jane" because that's what she became to me, one of my surrogate Road Trip Mamas. We keep in touch to this day. As for a low, my friend and I encountered some tension during my visit. I wasn't able to be present for and show up in the way that he had hoped. I found myself too wrapped up in my impending journey to enjoy his companionship. I have had regrets about that. With that said, I've also had to forgive myself. I was where I was at that point in my life and that's ok. Randall, please forgive me. Your kindness did my fragile heart good. Thank you.

May 15, 2012 (Los Angeles, CA)

Ah California, thanks for the vitamin D, the ocean water and the love. Flying back to Virginia tomorrow and feeling quite uneasy about the days ahead. I am open to the encouragement and support from all of the Angels in my Life. I can't wait to find out where I'm headed.

~Robin

*To tell you the truth, I don't even remember the flight home. I was that out of it. It all felt surreal.

May 16, 2012 (Los Angeles, CA)

If all goes as planned, I'll be on the road tomorrow evening. I'll update you on where I'm headed before I leave.

There are so many people that don't understand why I am doing this. Most times, I don't even have a clear understanding. That's ok, not required. What I do know is that my heart was aching and my Spirit cried out for more.

This is not just a Road Trip. This is a journey to restore that part of myself that has lost her Joy. This is a journey to reawaken my passion for living. This is a journey to nurture my Soul. This is a homecoming for the person that I was created to be.

I made the choice to take this trip in faith. I know and believe that all of my needs will be provided for along the way.

My plane back to Virginia leaves in a little over an hour. I'll be traveling all day but I'll check in with you tomorrow. Are you ready for a Road Trip? Alright then, let's get ready to do this. Thank you all so much for your support, I am very grateful.

To the upcoming Road Trip!

~Robin

May 18, 2012 (Suffolk, VA)

Fellow travelers! You thought I forgot, didn't you? Yesterday was indeed the 17th, better known as: the start of the Road Trip. Remember how I said "if all goes as planned?" Well, things haven't quite gone "as planned" and that's alright. I flew in from California last night and I was anxious to leave. My car, Zora the Honda, was having second thoughts. I spent yesterday giving her a bit of extra attention to get her in shape for the trip.

Tomorrow, however, is a new day.

To the Road Trip!

~Robin

*The next morning, the Road Trip was on the road. I had no idea which way to head so I went to the place that I was most familiar with and had last called home: the DC, Maryland, Virginia area.

May 19, 2012 (Washington, DC)

Fellow travelers! Sitting in the Howard University library (Free unlimited internet, sweet!), no particular place to call home and as happy as a clam. It's all good.

To the Road Trip!

~Robin

*And that's what I was trying to convince myself of, that it truly was "all good" even though it looked like anything but. A part of me was free and genuinely happy. The other part was terrified and questioning just what I had gotten myself into.

May 21, 2012 (Upper Marlboro, MD)

Fellow Travelers! This is technically day 5 of the Road Trip to Freedom. By now, I envisioned myself cruising along the open road, singing KC and the Sunshine Band, heading to meet ups with you all and savoring every moment of it. Now that's my kind of Road Trip!

Hold the phone, happy feet, not so fast. Here's how it went down.

Picking up my car and leaving VA was not the smoothest. I had to get my car from the shop (new brakes), renew my license (really, it expires today? Well played Universe), replace my cracked windshield and get the car inspected. And I had to do it on limited funds. Thanks to a $200 gift from a (mega-generous) friend and a repair shop IOU, I was on the road by the evening. Sweet freedom! While driving to my first stop in Maryland, I realized that I had forgotten my personal items. Toothpaste…who needs toothpaste?! This is a Road Trip! You do dear, trust me. Fine. I headed to Target, ran down the travel size aisle, grabbed one of everything and headed back to my car. Whew, mission accomplished. Time to get back on the road!

What my tired mind neglected to realize was that after I packed my items in my suitcase, I didn't put the bag back in the car. You heard me right folks, I left my suitcase in the Target parking lot.

I'm not a clothes gal by any means. With that said, half of the little that I did have, was gone. C'mon! I took a breath. I then made the choice to see it as a sign from the Universe telling me to: travel lighter. Point taken. Let's keep it movin'.

However, that was only the beginning of a set of mis-steps over the next few days.

Fast forward to 6am this morning. Woooo Hoooo, time to hit the road to NY! Slow down grasshopper, not so fast. The car wouldn't start. Say what? Are you serious? Really?!

I sat on the ground, had a laugh along with a few tears and proceeded to have a talk with the Universe. "What are you saying here? Is this a super bad idea? Should I not be doing this?" The answer I heard was clear, complete and to the point: Go. Don't get attached. Go.

Meaning, don't get attached to what it could or should look like. Instead, be open to what shows up.

This trip has looked nothing like I expected...and that's ok. For every mis-step, there have been ten times as many blessings that have come my way. For that, I am grateful.

Thanks to my kind cousin, the car is running again (nice!) and I feel led to New York and Pennsylvania in the next couple of days. Hang in there with me. We'll get this Road Trip on the road soon.

To the Road Trip!

~Robin

As comical as that may have sounded, losing that suitcase truly hurt my heart. I didn't take much with me, only the items that really meant something to me. And in a matter of seconds they were gone. That was one of those nights where there simply weren't enough curse words.

May 22, 2012 (Washington, DC)

Fellow travelers, I just got invited to stay at a B&B in the Adirondack Mountains of NY. Yes!

To my first official stop on the Road Trip!

~Robin

I don't quite remember how or why but I found myself back at the Howard University library. Again. While there, I posted on my Road Trip page that I was headed up North. I asked if there was anyone that had space for a traveling gal. Just as I was about to pack it in for the night, I got a response from a woman in New York. She said that she owned a B & B in the Adirondack Mountains and that I was welcomed to stay there for a few nights. Say what? Yes! And with that, I was headed to New York. The Road Trip to Freedom was officially on the road.

May 23, 2012 (Keene Valley, NY)

Fellow travelers, I know what it feels like to run away from something. This feels different. This trip is not about running away, hiding or leaving anything behind. This trip is about exploring, embracing and discovering my own path. This fits. It feels right.

Safe and sound at a welcoming, full of love B&B in Lake Placid up in the Mountains! I'm a tired gal. A happy gal, but a tired one. I have a fireplace, a kitchen and a bed big enough to get lost in. The owner was kind enough to lend me a laptop for the evening so that I could connect with my fellow travelers and let you know that all is well. I have officially made it to my first official destination, the Adirondack Mountains in New York! Do you know what the best part about it is? The B & B that I'm staying at is owned by one of you all!

Do you know what is also incredible to me? This lovely woman, along with so many others of you, have opened your hearts to me and offered your homes to me should our paths ever cross. To *me*, Robin. A soul that you have *never* met but that you have connected to for one reason or another. I can't even begin to describe how beautiful of a feeling that is. Thank you so much for that.

Headed to bed, friends. Goodnight everyone. Thanks so much to all my Angels (you know who you are) that have gotten me this far. I couldn't do this without you.

I do want to share one thing that I learned today: Just because I don't always feel strong, courageous and wise, it doesn't mean that I'm not. I am and so are you. Even in those times when we don't always feel that way, we are.

To the Road Trip and to resting well.

~Robin

My Angels were the people from the Road Trip to Freedom page. People that barely knew me or only knew of me from the year that we had spent together on my Choose Happiness page. Many wrote to me that they had been encouraged by my Choose Happiness posts and they now wanted to support me on my own journey to Happiness. I was humbled and grateful each and every time I received a gift along with a note of encouragement. "Robin, here is $10, enjoy lunch on me. Thank you for inspiring me to follow my own path."

May 24, 2012 (Keene Valley, NY)

Fellow travelers, I'm a happy gal.

~Robin

My first day in the Adirondack Mountains in my standard Road Trip attire: coveralls and my favorite cap turned to the back. You'll see this look again, trust.

*Why was I so happy? Perhaps it was because I was around people who actually enjoyed my presence. Or maybe it was because I could finally take a deep breath without feeling overwhelming anxiety in every part of my body. More than likely though it was simply that in that moment I was in a peaceful space, sharing time with a kind person and I was grateful about that.

May 25, 2012 (Keene Valley, NY)

Fellow travelers, still a happy gal. Just feeling a bit directionless and emotional at the moment. I'm packing up to leave the Adirondacks tomorrow. It's not so much about where I want to be today, I can go anywhere. I've been in a place that was so full of the love the past couple of days and I want to keep that feeling. I'm going to follow my heart, I'm so curious to see where I land.

This feels good.

To the Road Trip!

~Robin

My last day in the Adirondack Mountains. While I was sitting in this space, I didn't spend a minute wondering what was next. Instead, I allowed myself to enjoy that right then moment.

May 25, 2012 (En route to "I'm open to suggestions")

Fellow travelers, one more thing: the next time I mention the word "Road Trip", sit me down and lovingly shake some sense into me. I'll thank you for it later.

Leaving my temporary home among the mountains and I'm still unclear where I'm headed; next or ever. I think I have enough gas to make it to Vermont. We shall see. It sounds like a laid back place and since I've never been, why the flip not? Although it has been uncomfortable not knowing what's ahead, there is also an inexplicable feeling of freedom that comes along with it. Huh, guess I truly am going to get my Road Trip to Freedom.

To what awaits!

~Robin

May 26, 2012 (Brooklyn, NY)

Fellow travelers!

After leaving the stunning Adirondack Mountains yesterday, I was planning on having lunch at a cool hippie hang out in Vermont. Instead, I ended up having grilled cheese with my 93 year old Great Aunt in Connecticut and then Chinese food at 2am in New York City. That was one grilled cheese and conversation that I wouldn't have passed up for anything, and I don't even eat cheese. Now I'm in, oh shucks, who knows. Let's go with Brooklyn.

Also, many thanks to my surrogate Road Trip Mama for the midnight pep talk. I'm not a whiner but I needed to whine for a minute. All better now. Onward and upwards!

To the Road Trip!

~Robin

*That was the beauty of the trip. I was on my own time and it was about what was important to me right then. In that moment, I wanted to go see my cousins and my Great Aunt Jet and that was exactly what I did. Her health was not well.

Her family said that she was waiting to see the next set of twin great-grandchildren that were due here at any moment. Gratefully she was here to welcome them on the planet. She passed a year later. While at her memorial, I thought back on that day and smiled with thankfulness at the time that we had spent together.

May 27, 2012 (Harrisburg, PA)

Fellow travelers!

I'm already ready to go home.

Sorry tiny grasshopper, not yet.

So here's the deal: I'm headed to Michigan. Why Michigan? A fair question. A friend of mine messaged me and said that she had just moved into a new home and her previous home was just sitting there. Empty. She offered her space for me to stop for a while, rest and stay as needed. Say what? Michigan here I come!

To the Road Trip? We'll see about that...

~Robin

*Although I kept proclaiming that I could "go anywhere", the truth was that I was only going where there was "space" for me. Looking back on it now I realize that I was still traveling with a limiting perspective.

May 28, 2012 (Columbus, OH)

Fellow travelers, still on the road! Stopped for the night and I found an available computer at the library. That's been a challenge to do the past couple of days. I should be in Michigan tomorrow. I'll post more once I'm settled. I need some rest, it's been a long day. See you all soon.

To the Road Trip!

~Robin

May 29, 2012 (Lansing, MI)

Fellow travelers, wait a minute, what's the date? Where am I? Is this real life?

These are a handful of the questions that flood my mind when I open my eyes and try to figure out where I am for the day.

Today, I am in Michigan.

During my handful of weeks on the road, I have learned what it means to be open to receive blessings, about giving without expectation of anything in return, about what it means to be cared for, about being connected, about planting "roots" and about what unconditioned love looks like.

In my mind this trip looked quite different. It was meet ups at every stop along the way and posting each evening about the lessons and a-ha moments of the day. It was a trip filled with adventure, grace and ease!

Instead, the majority of this trip has been about plain old basic survival. Do I have enough gas money? Where am I going to stay today? Do I really have to stay in my car another night? Robin, is this the best you can do for yourself?

One thing this short journey has been about is connection for me. At times in my life, I have felt so displaced and alone. During my travels, people have welcomed me into their homes with love and genuine excitement. Many of you all didn't even know me. We have sat on front porches and watched the sun set, hiked in the mountains, cried together over life lessons, shared home cooked meals and connected, heart to heart. It has been so nurturing. My Spirit needed that.

I will be in Michigan for a short while as I plan what's next. Plan? You're funny, Robin.

There is a lot of love and support on this Road Trip, it's a good feeling. I'm grateful.

To the Road Trip!

~Robin

Let me say a few words about "connection with others" and my past relationship to it: I run from it, it used to scare the crap out of me and I always felt as though I was a complete screw up in my attempts to do so. As a result, I quit trying. I sealed myself up in a bubble of isolation and convinced myself that I could live *there foreva'. "I don't need people, I'll get cats" I often thought to myself. However, there was a part of me that started to crave human connection. The journey gifted me the chance to truly open my heart to people and to share my authentic self with them. I now see that my time on the Road allowed me not only to connect to myself but to others as well. In an interesting turn, this was also the day that I received an extremely generous donation of $200. The first thing I did was to go purchase a cell phone so that I could be even more "connected" to the people that cared about me.*

May 30, 2012 (Lansing, MI)

Fellow travelers, time for a Road Trip rewind! I never did tell you about my time in the Adirondacks. See what had happened was…

I was in DC and I asked the Universe where to head next. Oh yeah, you can ask Her. And if you get still and listen, I guarantee you'll hear an answer. What did I hear: New York. New York, huh? Fantastic, I'm there!

I pulled out my New York contact list, headed to the Howard University library and began sending emails to find a place to stay while in the city. After an hour, I had nothing. With the short notice and Memorial holiday weekend, I was out of luck. Universe, are you sure you meant New York?

Just as I was about to call it a day, I saw a message come through my inbox: "I own a Bed and Breakfast in the beautiful Adirondack Mountains, you are welcomed to stay here!"

See how that worked out? Love it! The next day I headed up to the Snow Goose Bed and Breakfast in Keene, NY. It was said to be "a woodland sanctuary for body and spirit" and that's exactly what it was.

I must have been quite a sight to my host as I wandered in late that evening after a long day on the road. She welcomed me in and showed me to a cozy and comfortable room. I had only been there 10 minutes and I already didn't want to leave.

In the morning, the smell of a home cooked breakfast was the perfect way to wake up. I chatted with Amy, the owner, and the other guests over our meal. I smiled as I looked around the table. It was such a sweet moment. There was no tension or stress. No one was rushing to be anywhere other than right where they were.

Amy offered to show me the sights that day and I happily accepted. Not only was I looking forward to exploring the beauty of the mountains, but I was also grateful to have the opportunity to spend time with her and connect.

I felt like an observer the next few days that I spent there. I listened to the conversations, I watched the interactions of the people and I soaked in the stories of those that were kind enough to share them with me. I'm not a talkative person, but I found that I was even less so during my time there.

When I shared this insight with Amy, she offered me a beautiful thought: "Maybe this is your time to rest and restore. Maybe you don't have to "do" anything right now, just be. I liked that, it felt good in my spirit. I had numerous things planned to "do" on this Road Trip. However, I might just end up getting a lesson in how to "be" instead.

To the Road Trip!

~Robin

*Amy and I truly did form a bond. She was a writer as well. A handful of our mornings together were spent sitting across the table from each other as we drank tea and wrote. I cherished that time with her. To this day, I still think back on it and smile.

My first host on the Road Trip and new friend Amy.

May 31, 2012 (Lansing, MI)

Fellow travelers!

Goodness, what to do next? Creative ideas seem to have abandoned me at the moment.

And on a side note…

Oooooprah! Just because I can. Is anyone out there in the Chicago area and could you put me up for a couple of days? I have a meeting with Oprah. But don't tell her, I want it to be a surprise.

To the Road Trip!

~Robin

May 31, 2012 (Lansing, MI)

Fellow travelers, have you ever done something that no one understood but you knew you had to do it anyway? Have you ever made plans to do something that made no "reasonable" or "logical" sense but it didn't matter, your Spirit still wanted to do it?

I think that's where I am. There is nothing "logical" about this journey and I'm a-ok with that. Logical? Nope, that's not in Robin's Road Trip dictionary.

As I settle in to call it a night, I could use some words of wisdom and an encouraging pep talk right about now. Share some of your experiences with me. What did you learn? Would you do it again? I have to think about my own answers to this one…

Rest well all.

To the Road Trip!

~Robin

*In response to the question a fellow traveler posted this poem:

"If I could live my life again.
Next time, I would try to make more mistakes.

I would not try to be so perfect, I would relax more.
I would be sillier than I have been.
I would take fewer things seriously.
I would be less fastidious.
Accept more risks, I would take more trips, contemplate more evenings, climb more mountains, and swim in more rivers.
I would go to more places where I have not been, eat more ice cream and fewer beans.
I would have more real problems and less imaginary ones.
I was one of those people who lived sensibly and meticulously every minute of their life. Of course I have had moments of happiness.
But if I could go back in time, I would try to have good moments only, and not waste precious time.
I was someone that never went anywhere without a thermometer, a hot water bag, an umbrella and a parachute.
If I could live again, I would travel more frivolously.
If I could live again, I would begin to walk barefoot at the beginning of the spring and I would continue to do so until the end of autumn.
I would ride more merry-go-rounds, I would contemplate more evenings and I would play with more children.
If I could have another life ahead.

But I am 85 years old you see, and I know that I am dying."

~JL Borges

June 1, 2012 (Lansing, Michigan)

Fellow travelers!

Road Trip motto for the day: "Go for it. Because really, what's the best that could happen?" And, with that, I'm out.

To the Road Trip!

~Robin

June 1, 2012 (Lansing, Michigan)

Fellow travelers!

I met a body piercer last night and he thought I had a cool story and a big heart. So he pierced my nose for free. What in the hell kinda Road Trip is this?! Oh right, it's a Robin Road Trip. That explains it.

I also wanted to take a moment to say how grateful I am to all of you that have been supporting and encouraging me along the way. If you've made a love offering, hosted me for a few days, shared encouraging words or sent positive thoughts into the Universe for me, then I say many thanks to you! I could not have gotten this far without you, I appreciate you all.

Time to sign off for the day and start "planning" (oh that's cute) the next leg of the journey. Chicago seems to be calling me at the moment.

This has been quite the adventure so far and I can't begin to imagine what's ahead. Go out there and do something completely spontaneous and deliciously random just because you can. These are *your* moments, enjoy them.

To the Road Trip!

~Robin

June 2, 2012 (Lansing, Michigan)

Fellow travelers, feeling a bit discouraged today. Inspiring words are welcomed.

On a brighter note, there is a lot of bunny wabbit energy where I am now, it's nice. I like the company. We are equally unsure of each other but our relationship is slowly growing.

To the Road Trip.

~Robin

June 2, 2012 (Lansing, Michigan)

Fellow travelers, check in time, yo.

This is one of those Road Trip days that I could do without. I am feeling unsettled and my thoughts are unclear. I am longing for the comfort of my own home. I am craving the feeling of being grounded. Thinking back, I can't say that I've ever known what it feels like to be grounded in one place.

I woke up this morning and had a complete "what are you doing?!" moment. It was not my finest moment. I looked around at my makeshift bed, glanced over at the suitcase that I've been living out of and then began to wonder how the $10 in my account (that I had been generously gifted) would be best put to use. In that moment, I was disappointed in myself. I was disappointed in my life. I was disappointed in every choice I had ever made.

People have often said that they wish they could just shake some sense into me. I now understand that sentiment. Let's see: I'm 30ish, no place to call home, pennies to my name and as aimless as they come.

However, here's the part that I don't understand: this is not me. This is in no way, shape or form who I was created to be. It's not me, I swears! But for some reason right now, it is.

Who am I? I am Robin. I AM creative, talented, motivated, intelligent, curious, innovative, capable, a visionary, perceptive, resourceful, understanding and aware. I know my own worth, I stand in my power and I live my purpose in each and every moment. I am LOVE! That's who I am.

And at the moment, not one bit of that is reflected in my life.

I'm beginning to understand that this Road Trip is giving me the opportunity to dig deep and do some heart work and healing. There will be many moments of joy and excitement, but there is more on the agenda as well.

I am on this journey to learn that I do belong here, to learn that I do have value and worth and to remember that I do matter. I am on this journey back to the me that I was created to be. I am on the journey to learn how to Love, appreciate and accept every aspect of who I am. Now that's what Robin's Road Trip to Freedom is all about.

For the moment, this is where I am. I'm learning to be ok with that. I'm doing my best and when (as Mama Maya Angelou says) I know better, I'll do better. I now choose to be gentle with myself and extend the same compassion and understanding to myself that I do to others. Today I choose to love Robin, right where she is.

This Road Trip not only gave me the chance to travel the country, it also gifted me the time to explore my inner landscape as well. So far, it's been quite a journey.

To the Road Trip!

~Robin

June 4, 2012 (Lansing, Michigan)

Fellow travelers, there is something about feeling forgotten that is intolerable to me. Dear life lessons, I hand picked you before I came here. I probably even did it with naive excitement. That conversation more than likely went like this: "Ohhhhhh, abandonment issues, you seem juicy. We're gonna get a whole lotta of healing done this time around. C'mon over here, you!" I get it.

With that said, I am now open to learn what you have to teach me. Soon or sooner would be lovely.

Thankssomuch.

To the Road Trip!

~Robin

June 5, 2012 (Lansing, Michigan)

"One's destination is never a place but a new way of seeing." ~ Henry Miller

And that's the truth, Ruth.

Figured out where I'm headed. That's progress. I'll take it! But before we get to that…

…A few years ago I was in a Spiritual Life Development Program. I didn't complete the program but my classmates that stayed are about to graduate and I want to be there. Silver Spring, Maryland here I come! I'll be on the road in a few days, give or take a day. I'll keep you posted.

600 miles. I can do this.

To the Road Trip!

~Robin

*The program that I had attended was meant to be completed in two years. For ten long years (off and on) I attempted to finish the course and never quite made it. I was insistent on going back although I could not wrap my head around why. It wasn't until after the Road Trip had ended that my unrelenting determination to be there made sense. I'll explain later. With that said, what I learned from the experience was that I am always perfectly placed wherever I am for a reason. Be alright where you are without being focused on the "why," that will come.

June 9, 2012 (Somewhere in Pennsylvania)

Fellow travelers, en route to the East coast to see my former classmates graduate! Thanks to my generous friends Teena, David and Coach Robin, I was able to get 450 miles in gas and tolls paid for, thank you! Only 150 more to go. I think I'm in Pennsylvania, who knows. I'll get there. Or not. Class of 2012, I'll see you soon, love you all! Thanks everyone.

And before I go: A big thank you to Staci, Randall, Jane, LaKeisha, Cousin Ivan and his family, Sharon, Mia, Elizabeth Anne, my Connecticut family, Pamela, Ingrid, Teena, David, Coach Robin, Amy C., Amy M., Amy K., Jenn, Anette, Kimberly, Chey, Shelby, Karen and the peeps over at Choose Happiness and Robin's Road Trip to Freedom! This is possible because of you, I am so grateful. Again, many thanks.

To Completion!

~Robin

*I never let a day on Road Trip come to a close without stopping to send up gratitude for all the people that were supporting my journey. Often it looked like pulling over on the side of the road, connecting with what I was feeling and sending up a shout of thanks. Some days it was just doing a quick happy dance in a parking lot. I had never in my life felt such kindness and compassion from others. I remember days where I just sat in my car and cried. However this time it was not out of sadness, but instead from a place of overwhelming thankfulness.

June 10, 2012 (Hellertown, Pennsylvania)

Fellow travelers, I'm having a random Road Trip moment. Feel free to share in it with me…

No, no, no, no, no, I don't want to get left behind in life! I don't wanna be an option! "If I make it fine. If not, then that's ok too." Hold on, not ok! But here's the thing, it ain't about other people, it's about me. I have to choose to stop leaving myself behind and making Robin an option. I can't expect anyone else to care one green jellybean about my life if I don't. So here's the deal: I care. I care! I'm going to stand up for ME because I'm worth it and *I* care! What does that look like? Yeah, don't know. Not important. Just wanted to let the Universe know that I'm still here. And I care.

I'm done. Needed to get that out. Thanks for sharing in my random moment. In other news, I'm still on the road to Maryland.

To the Road Trip!

~Robin

June 11, 2012 (Silver Spring, MD)

Fellow travelers, this week I took a detour and I'm back on the East coast to attend the graduation of my good friends.

For the past 10 days I've been in Michigan. I was given the opportunity to stay in one place for a little while and I said a resounding, YES thank you! I didn't do a lot. I sat on the steps and fed the wild rabbits. I went for walks and watched the sunset. I cooked a meal and enjoyed it in the quiet of the space. I enjoyed the moments.

On the flip side of that, what I didn't do was get too comfortable. Although I wasn't being rushed out, I never unpacked my suitcase. I kept my things in my car because, you know, you just never know. I never quite settled in. I was in this welcoming and peaceful space but there was this familiar discomfort that I became aware of.

The voices in my head were loud and relentless: Don't get cozy, grasshopper, this isn't your space. Enjoy it while it lasts because you'll never have your own home again. You'll be on a Road Trip foreva'! Well now, aren't you a killjoy?

I had to sit down and have a heart to heart with myself. C'mon Robin, what is this? Where is your faith and trust? Where is the belief that you are worthy and deserving of all things good? Where is the thought that you can do this? I searched my heart and scanned my body. It wasn't there.

However, there was this other part of me that I felt rise up. It was a small part, but she was there. Her voice was clear and steady. "Say what? You don't trust yourself? Look at all that has happened and you have *still* gotten yourself to this right now moment! You aren't worthy of love? Why are you still telling that ridiculous lie? Just the fact that you are here makes you worthy of love from others, just like everyone else! No, no, no, I know I didn't hear you say that you *can't* do this? Oh, yes. Yes you can. This process has broken you down in places, Robin, but it will not break you. Build your foundation on this. YOU build it. You don't need anyone to do it for you, you already have the tools. I know the sadness in your heart, it's ok. Remember that you are so loved and wrap yourself in that when you forget. You are *so* loved. Be kind to yourself, acknowledge yourself, honor yourself. Accept your perfectly imperfect self right where you are. Not where you want to be, but right where you are. I believe in you."

I took a breath and the tears started to fall. They were not fresh tears. They were tears from unexpressed hurts and disappointments of the past. I have reached a point where I am ready, able and available to begin healing my heart. This journey is turning out to be much deeper than I ever expected. For that, I am grateful. Take care everyone, see you soon.

To the Road Trip!

~Robin

June 13, 2012 (Silver Spring, MD)

Fellow travelers, still in the MD/DC/VA area for the day while I plan what's next. Anyone wanna get together? And thank you to LaKeisha for the hospitality, laughs and good ol' quality time. Tammy for the conversation, my handcrafted Choose Happiness talisman and the best vegan crab cakes eva' and Pamela for getting me refueled and fed, thank you! I had the biggest veggie chili dog ever seen in life in your honor.

To the Road Trip!

~Robin

*LaKeisha was a friend from the Spiritual Life Development program that I attended a few years back. I don't know if she actually knows what a huge impact she had on Robin's Road Trip to Freedom. To start, when I left for the Road Trip I had a map, a yellow highlighter and a handful of library printed Mapquest directions to find my way. When my friend learned this, she insisted that I take her GPS system to help navigate the way. She also introduced me to Dollar Tree. "Everything is literally a dollar" she said. That was the most priceless piece of Road Trip information anyone could have told me. Finally, she made sure I was well stocked with paper towels, a first aid kit, mini packets of detergent and other items that she thought would make my journey more comfortable and gentle.

The handmade keychain that my friend Tammy made for me. They said: Choose Happiness, I am Light and I am Enough. Those words got me through many tough days. I treasured her gift and I carry it with me to this day.

June 14, 2012 (Silver Spring, MD)

Fellow travelers!

Moms are good. I should get one.

In other news, I'm bringing my time in Maryland to a close and headed to Pennsylvania tomorrow. I'm going to hopefully meet up with some Road Trip peoples to hang out. Pennsylvania, the peaceful road warrior is on the way!

To the Road Trip!

~Robin

June 15, 2012 (Hellertown, Pennsylvania)

Fellow travelers!

We meet again Pennsylvania. In town for a meet-up with some of you all. Come on out and give the kiddo a hug to take back on the road.

To the Road Trip!

~Robin

Pennsylvania, I'm gonna work on that smile request. No promises.

June 16, 2012 (Hellertown, Pennsylvania)

Fellow travelers!

Had an awesome day with my Facebook friend Amy and her family today, you all are the best! In Hellertown, PA at the moment after the first Meetup of the Road Trip. We met at Amy's Scrapbooking store and had a night filled with arts n' crafts and connection. I'm wondering what kind of wonderfulness today will be filled with? I'm curious to see and to find out where I'm headed! Could be anywhere with the way this puppy is unfolding. Still with me?

On second thought, looks like I'm not far from New York. That settles it, I'm going to New York City! If you don't hear from me again then I've been discovered and I'm off to be a broadway star. As always, open for a place to rest my travelin' self for the night and budget friendly vegan eats. That sounds like an oxymoron. Thanks for the hospitality and love, Pennsylvania. City of apples, I'm coming for you!

To the Road Trip!

~Robin

June 17, 2012 (New York, New York)

Fellow travelers and New York City, I am here! I'm having dinner later on with someone. I wonder who it could be? I have no idea. Sounds good to me!

To unknown dinner dates in NYC!

~Robin

Soon after posting, a friend messaged me and jokingly asked if I was going to propose dinner to a stranger on the street. I replied, "Actually, I might!" and I meant it. I was in such a space of allowing at this point of the journey. I knew things would unfold just as they were meant to and I sat in excited anticipation of what and who was ahead. As it turns out, a friend invited me to dinner later that evening. As I sat across the table from my divined dinner date, I was so in the moment and in such a state of aliveness that it almost did not feel real.

June 17, 2012 (Secaucus, NJ)

Fellow travelers,

While in NY I had an offer to stay with a friend across the water in New Jersey. I'm grateful to say that I'm safe and sound for the night and feeling loved. Thanks to everyone for helping me get here. See, good vibes and thoughts do work! G'night folks.

To the Road Trip!

~Robin

Often I look back on my posts and it makes the journey seem simple and effortless. I'm in New York City one minute and then in the next I'm magically in New Jersey with a friend. In reality, I sat in a Whole Foods in New Jersey for three hours using their free wifi to make calls, send texts and put up posts in an attempt to find a safe space for the night. Many of my days were spent this way; waiting for that text, call or Facebook post to say: "please come, I have space for you…"

June 18, 2012 (The Jersey Shore)

Fellow travelers, Check in time!

At the moment, I'm down near the Jersey Shore. I'm not sure why. Anyway, one thing I've learned about New York is this: "adopt the pace of nature" is not their motto. I went from the Zen peacefulness of the Pennsylvania Dutch country to the "woah, what in the hell?!" of New York City. It was quite an adjustment.

As I reflect back on the trip, I realize that I've visited and stayed with over 30 people in the last month. That is incredible to me. I had the opportunity to spend time with family members that I haven't seen in years and new friends that I probably wouldn't have met had I not been on the trip.

At some point during our visit, they all ask the same question: "Just what exactly are you doing?" Once I begin hearing a question at least once a day, I start to actually give it some thought. I'm thankful that the people whose paths I've crossed have loved me enough to gently call me out when I'm not facing, accepting or telling the truth. That's a fair question. What am I doing? I continue to ask people to offer support but what are they supporting? A cross country joy ride just 'cause? Hold on lemme check…no.

Oh, and consider this your heads up: this is going to be an "extended" post. Don't say I didn't warn you.

Ok then! Let's do this. A month and a half ago I was living in a place that was not a good fit for me. It wasn't about anyone else, it was me. I wasn't happy. Actually, I was in a paralyzing state of fear and depression that had me feeling hopelessly stuck. Same thing. You would think that feeling that way would motivate me to get up off my butt and make a change. Nah bruh. I wasn't stuck but I felt as though I was. My thoughts were unclear, my body felt worn down and I was having deep feelings of despair. Those of you on the Choose Happiness Facebook page probably saw that reflected in my writing. I was not in my happy place.

My prayer was always the same: "Universe, I desire to move forward but I'm unclear how. Please make a way." Wouldn't you know it, two weeks later I was told to leave. Hold on, I think I got what I asked for. With that said, I didn't expect to get it quite that way. Maybe I should have been more specific. There I was: no place to go, no income, $20 to my name and zero motivation to do better. In other words: homeless. Damn, for real? Now if that isn't a recipe for all kinds of not nice then I don't know what is.

Here's what I have learned about Life, it's not about what happens. It's how I choose to respond to what happens. My first thought was fear, then disappointment, then panic and then a curious sense of calm. I sat myself down and had a heart to heart: "Ok kiddo, you've made some choices that have brought you to this place. There is a lesson here for you. I don't know what in the hell it is but it's there. This is an opportunity for healing. Embrace it. What's done is done, don't beat yourself up. Learn from it. Make a new choice. Move forward. Done."

Done, that's it? That's right folks, done. Let me keep it real. There are still conversations and healings that need to take place around the past few years. But as far as wallowing in what I did or didn't do, should or shouldn't have done, that's done. I'm complete.

Alrighty then. So how'd you end up on a Road Trip?

I was speaking with a friend about the situation and something she said sparked an idea. Instead of being passive about this and begging people "sweet peas and cream, can you *pleaaaseee* take me in for a couple days?" I made a new choice. I made the choice to go on a Road Trip. Robin's Road Trip to Freedom, that is. It's about where *I* want to go, how *I* want to get there and when *I* want to go. It's all me, baby. For the longest time I've felt like I was only here to accommodate other people. My job was to bend and mold to fit their needs and to stay out of the way. I lost me in the process. I'm sorry, Robin who? Don't know her.

Back to the original question, why am I on a Road Trip?

Right. My intention is to take the lessons that I have learned and share them with others who have been where I am and don't know "where" to go. I want to be an example of what it looks like to live in complete trust of the Universe. *Complete trust.* I want people to see me and remember that life is limitless and we can *always* make a new choice.

That's what Robin's Road Trip to Freedom is all about. It's about Truth, Freedom, Faith and Trust. When you support me in any way, that is what you are giving towards. My hope is that I can one day offer support to someone else on their own Road Trip to whatever quality in life they are in search of. As for me, I'm in search of Freedom from anything that limits me from living the joyful and purposed Life that I was intended to live. Fellow travelers, what's your journey about? And here's the thing about a journey, you don't actually have to go anywhere to have one. You know what I'm sayin'?

To the Road Trip!

-Robin

June 19, 2012 (New York, New York)

Good beautiful morning fellow travelers! Last night I headed back to the new found familiarity of New York to stay with a friend. Check out my view from the Upper West side of New York from my friends apartment. Today feels like a day full of adventure! Now that's my kinda day, care to join me?

On a side note: that thing you've always wanted to do? Yeah, that one. Go for it.

To the Road Trip!

~Robin

Most days when I woke up, I had no clue what city I was in. This was not one of those days.

June 20, 2012 (New York, New York)

Fellow travelers!

During my stay in New York, I've spent time with a newly ordained Minister who is a complete ball of joy and light. I've stayed with an awesome friend who was a professional dancer and has the most fantastic stories! I chatted with another friend (love you Ingrid!) over veggie dogs and cherished every moment of it. I've met a beautiful and brilliant woman from the corporate world that is making a shift and following her heart. And I had the opportunity to see a phenomenal spoken word poet and singer that made me have all kinds of feels. Shucks, do I really wanna leave? Yeah, no.

To the Road Trip!

~Robin

June 20, 2012 (New York, New York)

Fellow travelers, I could use a bit of soul soothing at the moment. I feel my time in New York is coming to a close and I'm unclear on where to head next. And that's alright.

This Road Trip has not been at all what I expected, but in a good way. I expected Meet-ups with you all, a camera full of pictures and an adventure that I could hardly keep up with! Really? Ha! No. I would sit down to plan a meet up and it was a challenge to get it to come together. I take out my map to see where everyone is and the peeps from the page are as spread out across the states as could be! I finally get one scheduled (yes!) at my friend Amy's store...and no one came. That's not exactly true. Amy owns a Scrapbooking store and she was having an open house and a midnight crop that same night. The people that were there, were there for that. However, there were a few folks that were fans of the page and knew who I was. I'll take it! At some point during the night I had the opportunity to sit and connect with one of them. We talked and shared. She told me what the page had meant to her and it touched my heart. I expressed my gratitude while doing my best not to get sappy. It was a beautiful moment. It was then that I once again realized what this trip is about: Connection. True and genuine human connection.

I'm still going to plan larger get togethers along the way but I'm also going to shift the focus a bit. When I get to your town, I really want to connect. One on one and heart to heart. I want to hear your dreams, your challenges and what brings you joy. I want to share mine with you as well. I want us to sit outside with a cup of tea and enjoy the moment. This journey has a foundation built on Love and I am experiencing that more each day. I am so grateful. With that said, this is still a Road Trip and I do want to share all of the wild and incredible moments I've had so far! It's in the works, I'm on it. Thanks so much for being my traveling companions along the way. Put on some tea, I'll be there soon.

To the Road Trip!

~Robin

June 21, 2012 (Edgewater, New Jersey)

Fellow travelers!

Ok, so what am I doing in Jersey? Again. All of my intuitive friends, any ideas? Or just make up something. Either way, I'm open. I'm having a total mental road block at the moment. Sitting here patiently listening for the next step. Wait, did you hear that? Exactly. Me neither. Ok, Whole Foods in Edgewater New Jersey, what message do you have for me? I'm all (non GMO corn) ears.

To the Road Trip!

~Robin

In response to that post a fellow traveler wrote: "I don't know, Robin....I kinda see a hot day...sitting on the stairs of a tired old house by the lonely dusty road.... playing the blues......watching a hay bale rolling by......drinking lemonade and feeling the buzz of a fly or two.... Sometimes time has to stand still, one needs to meditate and just BE...... you dig?"

Yes, my friend, I can dig it. I can so dig it.

My contemplative view from New Jersey

June 21, 2012 (Edgewater, NJ)

Fellow travelers!

Still unclear where to head so I'm just gonna get on the road. Jersey, I'm out! If you don't hear from me again then I've gone off to become the newest cast member of an MTV reality show.

Onto the next city wherever that may be.

To the Road Trip!

~Robin

June 21, 2012 (Loganton, PA)

Fellow travelers, according to the GPS, I'm in Loganton, PA. Good to know. Is this near anyone? Any ideas on where I should head next? As always, I'm open for suggestions.

To wherever I'm headed!

~Robin

*There were numerous times when I truly had no idea where in the hell I was. When that happened, I'd put up a post like this and see what showed up. Sometimes I was only a short ride away from a familiar face. Other times I unknowingly was in a place that was not the friendliest. More than once a fellow traveler would gently attempt to give me a heads up on just where I was. I once received a private message saying "Hey there! I see you're in (insert city). I've spent time there, interesting place! You may want to head to the next town over before you call it a night, it's more traveler friendly. Stay safe. To the Road Trip!"

The people that joined me on the journey looked out for me from behind their computer screens. I later learned that many of them would log in to Facebook to watch out for my update at night just to make sure I was somewhere safe for the evening. They genuinely cared. They will never how much that meant to me.

My "I'm not sure where in the hell I am" face. You'll see this face again, yep.

June 22, 2012 (Boardman, OH)

Fellow travelers!

Resting for a moment at the Flaming Ice Cube Vegan Café & Shoppe in Ohio. The Flaming Ice Cube, that's a paradox. I like. 30 days, 5000 miles and the only incident was that I ripped my nose ring out last night. Send bandaids, a mix tape from 1985 and a box of Apple Jacks. That's pretty damn good if I do say so myself.

To the Road Trip!

~Robin

June 22, 2012 (Freedom, OH)

Fellow travelers!

I'm in a city called Freedom, I love that. Spent the past day making my way through Ohio and now I think I've got it: first stop Michigan and then Chicago, Canada, Oregon and New Hampshire. Not so much in that order but whatever works. Whew, took a sec to get clear.

To the Road Trip!

~Robin

During the week after I left New York, I meandered around Pennsylvania and Ohio and then headed back to Lansing, Michigan. Michigan ended up being somewhat of a "home" base for me twice during the trip. And with that, I was headed back to the empty house that I had called home a few weeks before.

June 23, 2012 (Lansing, Michigan)

Fellow travelers!

The peaceful Road Warrior is home for a little while. It's not a permanent space, but for now, I am home. I can unpack, take a breath, get grounded, create a safe space, write, rest and cook a meal. I'm a happy and grateful gal.

To the Road Trip!

~Robin

June 26, 2012 (Lansing, Michigan)

Fellow travelers, I'm still here! I seem to have no sense of time on the road. If you've seen me along the way then you know that I'm constantly asking "just what day is this, exactly?"

I'm in Michigan and so grateful to have down time. I needed this, I was tired. I can't even tell you when I got here but I can tell you that I've been asleep for 2-3 of those days. When I haven't been sleeping, I've been writing. Sleep, write, sleep, write, sleep, write. You get the idea.

Thank you all so much for the Love, support and encouragement! I couldn't do this without you.

And when you get a moment, please send positive thoughts, mind bending books and socks.

To the Road Trip!

~Robin

*There were times on the Road Trip when I evaporated. Thin air. No posts. No calls. Anyone seen Robin? During those times I felt as though every bit of me had been expended and that I didn't have anything left to give or share. This was one of those times. However, there was one message that I did respond to. A former teacher that I was connected to via Facebook reached out and asked me to dog sit for her. It would mean another place to stop and rest. In two weeks time I would be headed back to Pennsylvania.

July 5, 2012 (Bloomsburg, PA)

Fellow travelers!

I've missed you! I've been away for a bit but I'm still here. Need to just be for a minute and breathe.

Just arrived in Pennsylvania to pet sit for a friend. I'll be taking care of her three sweet, lovable black labs. If you know me at all then you know I'm more of a cat person. I don't dislike dogs, I just really like cats. I'm also not big on cleaning up after anyone but myself. Growth will be happening, of that I am certain. This should be an interesting couple of weeks for us all. Send patience, love and doggie treats.

To the Road Trip!

~Robin

July 6, 2012 (Bloomsburg, PA)

Fellow travelers!

I want to be as loved, as well fed and sleep as good as the three doggies I'm taking care of. Me and three big ol' cuddlebugs that just want to snuggle. I'm already in love with them. I wish you could feel how sweet this is.

To puppy love!

~Robin

I honestly did begin to enjoy my time with the dogs. Aside from food and quality time with a tennis ball, they expected nothing from me. They loved me as is. That was one of the most caring experiences I had during my time on the Road Trip.

July 7, 2012 (Bloomsburg, PA)

Fellow travelers!

Someone just told me that my current experience of lack and limitation is because I'm having feelings that are, let's say, the opposite of warm and yummy. Hot damn, that would be accurate. I'm not a fan of myself at the moment. Time to bring on the Self Love. I can't give to anyone else what I am unwilling to first give to myself. Word.

To Self Love!

~Robin

July 8, 2012 (Bloomsburg, PA)

Fellow travelers!

Hmmm, Robin with a pair of hair clippers and a heaping amount of chocolate available to me. That rarely ever ends well. Screw it, let's do this! I'll send pictures.

To a new do!

~Robin

Road Trip homemade haircut 2012. Not too shabby if I do say so myself.

July 13, 2012 (Bloomsburg, PA)

Fellow travelers!

Someone just looked at the Choose Happiness bumper sticker on my car and smiled. It's official, I have changed the world.

To doing what you can where you are.

~Robin

My own personal creations: Choose Happiness bumper stickers.

July 14, 2012 (Bloomsburg, PA)

Fellow travelers!

This is my last day of dog sitting and tomorrow I'm back on the road. To celebrate, how about a little Robin's Road Trip to Freedom Q & A!

Is the Road Trip still going on? Yesssir!
Where are you? Pennsylvania.
Do you know where you're headed? Hmmm, I was going to ask you.
Are you back on track and feeling good? I'm back on track. The good feels are on the way.
For real? For reals.
Are you learning anything along the way? I am!
Are you doing anything with it? Shucks to the yes! Stay tuned, I'll keep you posted…
And with that, it's time to get this Road Trip back on the road.

Love and gratitude to you all.

To the Road Trip!

~Robin

July 15, 2012 (Bloomsburg, PA)

Fellow travelers,

Got it! On the way to Rhode Island.

To the Road Trip!

~Robin

July 15, 2012 (Dupont, PA)

Fellow travelers!

Hold the phone, the Universe had a change of plans for me: Atlantic City, here I come.

To the Road Trip. Again!

~Robin

Often it was a fleeting thought crossing my mind that led me to change directions. In choosing a destination, I never spent hours pondering where I should go and why. I just went. I just went. I knew that I couldn't get but so "off course" because wherever I was "supposed" to be was where I ended up.

July 16, 2012 (Atlantic City, NJ)

Fellow travelers!

Hello from Atlantic City! Ahhhh, the beach. And yes, it was as relaxing, peaceful and healing as it looks. While I was in New Jersey I did the tourist thing and headed to the Trump Tower Casinos. I'm not a gambler, but I am quite pleased to report that I won 75 cents. True, I spent $1 to get the win but why split hairs? It's a win! That made me think about how often I do that in life. I don't acknowledge a personal victory simply because it wasn't a "big" deal. No more of that! Going forward, I choose to recognize every accomplishment, every effort attempted and every baby step taken. It doesn't matter if I fall on my face over and over again. What matters is that I get back up. Job well done, Robin. Job well done, indeed.

What I have learned during this part of the journey is that I don't have to wait for anyone to encourage or appreciate the steps that I have taken.

I am more than capable of being my own cheerleader for the victories in my life, the big ones and the little ones. And when I think about it, there are no "little" victories. They are all meaningful. Goooo Robin!

After I left the beach, I felt a bit of an ache in my heart. I soon realized that it was because I missed my best friend. I had not seen her for over a year. And with that, I got in the car and headed to Maryland to give her a hug. That's how I roll on this Road Trip, I follow my heart. That's where I'm on the way to now and I couldn't be any happier. It's moments like these that make this journey priceless. Today was a good day.

To the Road Trip!

~Robin

Me and the hat in Atlantic City, NJ.

July 18, 2012 (Gaithersburg, MD)

Fellow travelers, Chipotle. Am I really getting ready to write a post about Chipotle? Yes, yes I am. This is odd for two reasons. First, I've never eaten there. And second, it's random.

I'm going to go with it.

Yesterday was a good day. I visited with my best friend ever in life and had time to emotionally recharge. Today however, is not the best. I'm grumpy. Zora the Honda is running on fumes. My clothes are dirty. I dropped my bag of Andy Capp hot fries. I had a friendship crumble. And I need a shower. I'm sure that's more than you wanted to know. I'm ok with that.

With that said, earlier today my friend and Sister in Spirit had a double mastectomy.

Wait. What was I complaining about? Oh that's right, not a damn thing. I'm not comfortable in this current situation. Big deal. I can only imagine what she is feeling in this moment. I don't have some of the basics of life that I have come to expect yet have shown so little gratitude for. My friend, on the other hand, has gone through this journey with such a spirit of thankfulness for each and every experience.

I have nothing to complain about. I have everything to be grateful for.

What does Chipotle have to do with this? I'm going to take the few dollars in my pocket, go get a meal there, park my car and then wait until I'm able to move forward again. Then I'm going to go dance in the rain and give thanks for the healing that is already taking place for my friend in her body and her Spirit. All is well, it always is. Even when it doesn't look like it or feel like it, all is well.

To the Road Trip.

~Robin

My first burrito bowl eva'. My love affair with Chipotle continues to this day.

*What I learned from this experience is that life, for the most part, isn't that serious. I've learned not to allow little inconveniences and annoyances to take my time, energy or focus away from what truly does matter. I'm grateful to say that my friend's body is now free from illness. She later told me that as a result of my Road Trip, she was inspired to embark upon her own journey once her chemotherapy was complete. Rev. Alicia, thank you for walking your path with such courage and grace. I love you.

July 19, 2012 (Rockville, MD)

Fellow travelers,

People are people, even the ones with labels. Doctor, Reverend, Counselor, Teacher, Mom and Dad. They make messes in life, they get their feelings hurt and they are still learning, just like we all are. People are people. Everyone is doing the best they can. Let's be gentle with each other.

And note to self: Quit trying to be around people that don't want to be around you. There are so many others that do enjoy you, go find them. I am complete with feeling tolerated, I now go where I am celebrated. I deserve that and so do you.

To the Road Trip!

~Robin

*This part of the journey was especially painful for me. I had developed a friendship with a woman a handful of years back. Although we were not far apart in age, she took on a "mother figure" role in my life. On the other side of that, I took on the "child/little sister" role in hers. She had a desire to nurture. I needed to be nurtured. For a while it worked, but over time the relationship began to shift. I experienced her as distancing herself and I was unclear why. When I asked her about it, she denied that anything had changed. Her words said one thing and her actions felt as though they spoke another. It didn't feel right. To be honest, I expected more from her. She was a well respected teacher in the Spiritual Community and I thought that made her "better" or smarter at life. I now know that's not true. As I said earlier, people are people and we're all here learning.

We disconnected while I was traveling, however I did reach out when I drove through her town. My sincere requests to connect felt dismissed. I felt rejected, again. "You used to want me around. Now you don't. Why? What's wrong with me?" This experience taught me two things. First, there is nothing wrong with me. Ever. And second, why people do what they do or don't do doesn't have a thing to do with me. She was playing out her own story in the same way that I was playing out mine. We had enlisted each other to play a part in this journey, that was all. There was healing for us both in the friendship and we showed up in each others' world for that reason. That experience taught me what it looks and feels like to be in a relationship of any kind and feel valued. For that and for her, I am grateful.

July 20, 2012 (Alexandria, VA)

Fellow travelers!

Clean clothes make me happy.

That's all.

So fresh and so clean, clean!

To the Road Trip!

~Robin

*As far as I can tell from this post, I had the opportunity to wash clothes. That was always a good reason to celebrate on the road.

July 21, 2012 (Aspen Hill, MD)

That's so sweet, thanks little fortune cookie.

I sought to find goodness in each day on the road. On that day it came in the form of a fortune cookie.

July 25, 2012 (Rockville, MD)

Fellow travelers!

Not being attached to how things are going to work out is a nice feeling.

To the Road Trip!

~Robin

*"Don't get attached" was a reoccurring theme along the way. Whether it was losing my luggage in the Target parking lot (I'm still salty about that) or thinking that I had a place to stay for the night then having it fall through, I always heard the same thing: it's still ok. Don't get attached, keep moving forward.

July 26, 2012 (Charlottesville, VA)

Fellow travelers!

Currently in Charlottesville, Virginia helping a friend move and start her own new journey. Last time I wrote a post, I was in Maryland visiting a friend. It wasn't until I had been there 4 or 5 days that I realized that I was...home. I was in the city that I grew up in and wasn't even aware of it. To me, it was just another stop on the Road Trip.

It was a blessing that (due to lack of funds) I wasn't able to hit the road as planned. Had it been up to me, I would have been outta there. Being in that place gave me the chance to get still and reflect on the past in a way that I had not done before. I ended up being thankful for the time that I had there.

Dear Universe, forgive me for doubting your ways, your plan is always for my good. I'm starting to understand that.

One lesson I learned while in Maryland: I might not be the person that I aspire to be, but I'm sure not the person that I once was. Everything is progress.

To the Road Trip!

~Robin

July 28, 2012 (Charlottesville, VA)

Fellow travelers,

Everyone deserves at least one place where they feel welcomed, comfortable and at home. Just my two cents from the road.

~Robin

August 1, 2012 (Silver Spring, MD)

Fellow travelers! Let's start with the basics:

Where am I? I'm in Maryland again. I did head to Virginia for a few days to help a friend pack but then I came back here. To start, I have a house sitting gig here this weekend and I didn't want to travel very far away. Also, funds are momentarily limited so I'm contained to 100 miles in any direction. Hey Universe, you can't contain the Road Trip to Freedom! Wait, She actually can. It's all good, there must still be learning here for me. I continue to hear the call of the road and I look forward to getting back on it. I've been getting vibes to head to Canada, Westward, Hawaii, down South and overseas. I'd say that narrows it down quite nicely.

Ok, to the post!

At least once a day, I ask myself the same question: Yeah, um, what happened Robin?

You weren't the brightest crayon in the box but you had potential, kiddo. And now look at you: On a so called "Road Trip", living out of your car and with no plan for how to make it better. Woah, you are so not the rockstar I thought you were going to be.

At this point, I go buy cookies. Then I find a bench to sit on so that I can re-evaluate every choice that I've ever made in life. Ever.

Ok, ok and ok! So I'm here and it looks really funky and I don't know how to "fix" it and I feel like I'm wasting my one precious life and that scares me!

After I finish my dramatic tirade to the Universe, I sit back down and eat the other cookie. Then I listen. And I wait.

I listen for a hint of what to do next. I look for a sign of confirmation that I'm at least close to the path that I'm destined to be on. Did you hear that? Crickets.

I actually have been hearing a message recently. However, it wasn't what I wanted to hear so I chose not to listen. If I don't acknowledge it then I didn't really hear it! Right? Not quite, Robin.

What I heard was this: "Be where you are, fully. Embrace the right now moment and know that you are perfectly placed. Be here. Now. Come present and know that this right now moment is your life. Breathe in the moment. Be here. Right here. Now."

That's it? Be here? Hold the phone, I want a life full of adventure, excitement and passion! I want to use up every bit of potential inside of me and live each moment on the edge, bring it!

And in response, I heard: Be here. Now.

What I have learned during this part of the journey is this: Although I crave an expanded existence right now, I have found that I'm being called into a reflective and still place in my life.

Oftentimes the most profound journeys are the ones that don't take us anywhere. Instead they allow us to explore our inner Universe. Wherever you are, be there fully. Be present to the experience. Open your heart to the lessons that the moments hold for you. And get a cookie. Cookies are always good for a journey.

To the Road Trip!

-Robin

August 2, 2012 (North Bethesda, MD)

Fellow travelers,

Any of my Facebook Mamas out there? Send Love.

To the Road Trip...

-Robin

August 3, 2012 (Olney, MD)

Fellow travelers!

I'm surrounded by Angels that look like people.

And speaking of people, I just talked to a woman that was completely convinced with all of her being that today was Wednesday. Oh good, I'm not alone.

To the Road Trip!

~Robin

One of the many acts of kindness I received along the way.

During a visit to Roots Market, I started a casual conversation with one of the employees. We ended up talking about my travels for a few minutes and then I continued on shopping. As I was about to check out, she came up to me with an entire bag filled with enough bath and body samples to last a month.

August 4, 2012 (Olney, MD)

Fellow travelers!

Still in Maryland at the moment and heading to Virginia tomorrow to housesit for a friend. I've been in hotel Honda for the past few days and my body aches. Gratefully looking forward to a bed tomorrow night. Rest well everyone.

To the Road Trip!

~Robin

Although I had kind and generous people that opened their homes to me along the way, there were still many nights spent in my faithful car, Zora. On those nights, the Holiday Inn Express was my saving grace. Their parking lots were well lit, the front desk staff were kind and the bathrooms were spotless. After a while, I got into a rhythm: I would find a space that was well lit but not too obvious, park and then go in to talk to the front desk. I was always honest. I told them that I was traveling, I didn't have money for a room and asked if it would be ok for me to rest in their parking lot and use their bathrooms. The majority of the time they said yes. Many of them even offered to keep a watchful eye out as I slept. I appreciated that. To this day Holiday Expresses have a special place in my heart.

August 5, 2012 (Alexandria, VA)

Fellow travelers!

Home sweet home (aka house sitting) for a week for a friend. Sweeeeet! The lady next door is cooking something delicious smelling. I think it's time to go make a new friend. In a perfect world she'd be watching Oprah's life class and I could join her for dinner, fellowship and a few a-ha moments. I'll keep my schedule open.

To new friends!

~Robin

August 6, 2012 (Alexandria, VA)

Fellow travelers, I'm going to do my best to keep this short and fluffy. However, this is me we're talking about. It could take a turn into the introspective and reflective at any moment. Be prepared.

Ok then! Let's do this.

Today I'm still house sitting for a friend in Alexandria, Virginia. I arrived here Sunday and I'll be leaving Friday. That's five days. Five whole days of a real bed, a kitchen, no searching for a shower, peace and quiet and an entire apartment all for me. For me! I am sharing it with the hippest cat on the planet named Leroy but we're both cool with it.

Here's the deal: I'm so excited about having a bed to rest well in, that I can't choose between sleeping all day or taking advantage of the quiet time and writing all day.

Today, I wrote. Tomorrow, I sleep.

What I realized while being here was this: I'm settling in my life. I am.

I was standing in the middle of a comfortable modest one bedroom apartment and I was in awe. I was amazed that someone could actually have an entire apartment all to themselves. I wanted to soak up every minute of my time in the space because I wasn't sure when I would get the opportunity to feel that way again.

Uh, when did this limited thinking come into my being? When did I convince myself that I wasn't worthy of my own space on the planet? When did I start to believe that I wasn't a capable adult that could create a comfortable life again?

So much for not being reflective and keeping it short and sweet. What can I say, I tried.

Here's what I've learned during my time here: I've been playing small and believing that I am less than and undeserving of the basics of life. Lies, all lies!

Universe, hear this: Today I affirm and claim my place here. I know that I am as worthy and deserving as all of the other sweet souls that I share this planet with. I now open my heart to receive all the love, JOY and goodness that you have for me. I thank you in advance for prayers that are answered before I even speak them and Blessings from unexpected sources. Thank you, thank you, thank you! I am so grateful.

You deserve to have all that your heart desires. So do I.

Friends, I am going to rest well tonight. I hope you do the same.

To the Road Trip!

~Robin

August 7, 2012 (Alexandria, VA)

Fellow travelers!

The blogging seminar in Chicago that I was waitlisted for just opened up. Wait, Chicago? That must be a sign. Harpo Studios, I'm on the way!

To Oprah, man!

~Robin

Although my funds appeared (and were) limited, I continued to make plans for the activities that interested me. One of those tentative plans was a seminar on blogging. Did I have the money to go? Nope. Did I still hold the Vision that I would be able to attend? Absolutely. One life changing lesson I learned on the road was that everything I desired to have began with the belief that I actually could have it. All that exists began as a thought. Want to have a new experience? Have a new thought.

August 8, 2012 (Alexandria, VA)

Fellow travelers, I feel as if I'm doing Robin's Road Trip to Freedom wrong but there is no wrong, right? It's more challenging at the moment than it needs to be. Calling in ease, grace, flow and abundance of all kinds today. There, that's better.

To the Road Trip!

~Robin

I think I was somewhere when I took this picture. Yep, I remember now, I was somewhere.

August 8, 2012 (Washington, DC)

Fellow travelers!

I just met a kind and kindred spirit at the meet up. Our conversation and time together really blessed me. Thank you for being, Dennis.

To connections!

~Robin

August 9, 2012 (Alexandria, VA)

Fellow travelers!

Can I call a Road Trip time-out?

My week of house sitting is complete and it's time to pack up and move on. I admit, there is some apprehension and fear around this next part of the journey. I feel clear on where I'm headed (Chicago) but I have no idea how that's going to happen. I've felt the stress of my wondering throughout the day. There is tightness in my chest, my hands are shaking and my attention span is nowhere to be found. Wait, what did you say? Where am I?

This is why I need a time out.

Even though I've only been traveling for 3 months, I realized that I've been on a Road Trip for years. Years, I tell ya'! I can't remember the last time that I felt settled and grounded. I can't recall a time when I wasn't trying to figure out my next move and counting the change in my pocket.

There is something very habitual about the way that I have been living. As I look back, I can see familiar and similar patterns in my slightly bent family tree. That being said, with all the gratitude and love in my heart, I now tell anything that does not exist for my highest and greatest good: to kick rocks.

And with that, I'm going to Chicago!

Thanks for the encouragement and support everyone.

To the Road Trip!

~Robin

August 10, 2012 (Alexandria, VA)

Fellow travelers!

I'm goin' to see Oprah, done. But, I need some time with a Mama for a little while. Who can I come see?

That's all.

To the Road Trip!

~Robin

I continued to learn how to be vulnerable and honestly ask for what I wanted during the trip. If I wanted quality time or a hug, then I let people know. My sincere requests were always met with understanding and kindness. From that post, I got a welcoming invite to spend time with a former classmate when I passed through Ohio. I did just that and it was exactly what I needed.

August 10, 2012 (Alexandria, VA)

Fellow travelers!

This woman just wrote me and said my Road Trip inspired her to follow her soul's calling and book a trip to Paris. And, it wasn't in her budget! I think that's outstanding. Budgets are good. They aren't everything. The Universe has her covered, no doubt.

To Paris!

~Robin

This was one of the numerous emails I received from fellow travelers thanking me for inspiring the courage within them to make a new choice and take a leap of faith. I was humbled and in awe each time I heard of someone "going for it" because of my own Road Trip to Freedom.

August 11, 2012 (Alexandria, VA)

Fellow travelers,

Today I'm back on the road! I'm leaving Virginia and headed to Chicago with a stop in Ohio. I don't think I have quite enough gas for the 8 hour trip so we'll see what interesting place I land in for the night. I know that the plan, even if it's not my plan, is always perfect.

To the Road Trip!

~Robin

August 11, 2012 (McArthur, Ohio)

Fellow travelers!

Made it to Ohio! Thought I had a place for the night but there was a bit o' miscommunication. Hey, it happens. Anyone live in the McArthur, Ohio area or know of somewhere I could stay for a night? I can still travel for another 2 hours if you're in a nearby city. See what I mean about making plans? But you know what, it's still all good! I believe that, thanks everyone.

To the Road Trip!

~Robin

August, 12, 2012 (Columbus, OH)

Fellow travelers,

Good beautiful morning everyone! I'm safe and sound in Ohio en route to Chicago. Thanks to one of you lovely people, I had a place to stay for the night. My host at the B&B earlier in the trip from New York messaged me and said that her son lived near there. And with that, I was headed to a welcoming home and fresh bagels in the morning. Thank you Amy, Christian, Angels and Universe!

This trip has truly taught me to hush up and listen. When I start trying to "figure out" where to go, then that's my cue to sit down, get still and listen. If at the moment, I don't hear anything, I wait. Then if needed, I wait some more.

I've stayed in "Hotel Honda" more times than I care to admit on this journey. Last night I was preparing to do that but something in my Spirit said "not tonight." I'm learning to not question the messages I hear from the Universe. I don't have to understand the "why" of the whispers that I hear. All I have to do is open my heart to receive it and say, "Yes, thank you." As a result, I was blessed to meet a kind and gentle Spirit last night. I'm grateful for that.

The same applies for this trip to Chicago. All I heard was the call to go. Are you sure Universe? Have you seen my PayPal account balance? Go to HARPO studios? In response to my inquiring mind, I heard: Go.

Well, alright then!

I'm in Ohio at the moment and 5 hours away from Chicago. Oprah is holding Lifeclass tomorrow night and I intend to manifest a seat in the audience. Can't wait to see how this one unfolds!

As always, good thoughts and words of encouragement are appreciated! Thank you everyone.

What I've learned during this part of the journey is this: Trust myself. Trust the process. Trust the journey. It's all for my good.

To the Road Trip!

~Robin

August 13, 2012 (Chicago, Illinois)

"I'm realistic, I expect miracles." ~Dr. Wayne Dyer

Road Trip reminder for the day: All things are possible. That thought that just crossed your mind? Even that one.

To possibility!

~Robin

August 13, 2012 (Chicago, Illinois)

Fellow travelers!

Made it safe and sound to Harpo studios in Chicago! Rainy but good trip. Took a bit longer because I kept stopping to look at shiny things along the way. Headed over to the studio now. Um, not sure to do what exactly but I'll figure that out when I get there. Story of this trip. Will keep ya' updated. Thanks for the well wishes everyone.

To the Road Trip!

~Robin

Standing outside of HARPO Studios with the intention of manifesting a ticket to Lifeclass.

August 13, 2012 (HARPO Studios)

Fellow travelers and Oprah Winfrey Network, I'm still here! No ticket yet but they don't tape for another six hours. I'll get the line going and see what happens.

To being patient!

~Robin

August 13, 2012 (HARPO Studios)

Fellow travelers, update: I'm in, wooooo hoooooo! I made it to Lifeclass at Harpo studios! Post coming later tonight.

What I learned on this part of the journey: All things really are possible.

To Lifeclass!

~Robin

August 14, 2012 (Chicago, IL)

Fellow travelers!

Ok folks, here it is: My Oprah post.

A couple of days ago I heard the call to head to Chicago. I let the Universe know that while there, I wanted to go to Lifeclass. Here's the deal: I had no plan, no tickets, no nuthin'. I arrived in Chicago at 2am yesterday morning and waited. Then I waited some more. At 8am, I saw a picture that my FB friend had posted...she was in the HARPO studios green room! She happened to be working as the assistant to the Lifeclass guest for that day. I took it as a sign. I messaged her, tagged her in a post, everything! The first show started taping and I still hadn't heard from her. I decided to leave Starbucks and head to the studio. During the walk there, I had a thought: maybe she got my messages and put my name on the guest list. I anxiously got in line with the ticket holders and waited my turn. No name on the list.

However, there was hope: I was on stand by. I'll take it! It was me, an incredible young man following his own dream (Avery Ford, check him out) and four ladies from Canada that were hilarious. We did our best to keep each other encouraged. "Yeah, of course we'll get in! Maybe." Another hour goes by and the HARPO employee comes out. "Ok, you're in!" We all shout with excitement and start heading back. "Hold on, not you two." She was talking to me and Avery. Say what? But we're so close! While we waited, we made the best of it and enjoyed each others company. Finally, the HARPO employee comes back out and tells us we're in but we won't have the best seats. We'll take it! We walk in the studio and I can't help but smile, it's happening. They take me to my seat and it's an incredible seat! Right in the middle, perfect.

The next couple of hours were surreal. We danced together, hugged, shared family secrets and just watched Oprah be Oprah. Did I get the picture I wanted? No. Did Oprah offer to mentor me and give me a place in the OWN family? Not this time. Did we sit down and bond over tea? Nope. However, something tells me that this was the first of our meetings together. All in good time.

The only thing nagging at me is that even after all that goodness and grace flowing my way, I still didn't believe that I could have what I wanted: a picture. What I wanted to do was stand in my chair and scream "OPRAHIWANTAPICTURE!" However, a part of me was still in doubt that I could have that. Still! Wow, the untruths that I tell myself even in the midst of magic and miracles.

I didn't have the big "O" moment but my Spirit is content. I followed my heart. I said all that to say: if there is something you want to do, do it. Don't sweat the details, let the Universe handle that. You can do it. You just have to believe you can.

One of the highlights, and there were many, was that I was also able to let down a wall. As a result, I made some new friends. What a gift.

That wasn't the story I was hoping to share but it is what it is. And what it is, is all good. Thank you, Universe. Thank you also for the encouragement and support everyone. It's been an incredible and happy day.

To the Road Trip!

~Robin

At HARPO studios in Chicago for a taping of Lifeclass with Oprah.

*Whenever I begin to doubt what a powerful creator I am, I think back on that moment. I had a Vision of what I desired and no idea how it was going to manifest. This experience taught me that knowing the details of how my request will unfold is not required. My job is to show up, hold the Vision and trust that it is already done.

August 14, 2012 (Chicago, IL)

Fellow travelers!

I'm off to explore Chicago with my current hosts and new friends. I met one of them in line waiting for the Oprah show so you know he's my kinda people! Go share a smile with someone that needs it. Enjoy the rest of this beautiful day, see you soon!

To the Road Trip!

~Robin

The Bean in Chicago. If you look closely, you can see a tiny sized version of me in it taking a picture.

August 15, 2012 (Chicago, IL)

Fellow travelers, good morning! I had a wonderful night in Chicago with my two new friends. We saw Millennium Park, Navy Pier, ate Chicago hot dogs with NO ketchup. The vegan kiddo only indulged in the smells but they looked delish! Then, we danced on the subway platform to two men singing oldies but goodies. "Stand By Me" was my favorite. Chicago, I love it here, thank you.

Last night I had such an incredible time and all I wanted to do was call someone and tell them about it. Let me tell the truth, I wanted to call home. I wanted to call home and share all of the fun and let them know that I had a safe and comfortable place for the night. I wanted to check in and let them know if I needed anything. I wanted someone to check in with me and see how I'm doing and to ask how my heart is feeling during the journey. But at the moment, there is no home to call.

I can't say that I want someone to care because there are lots of people that care. You all have been such a beautiful support system for me. I also have incredible friends that have loved me through this process, especially when I forgot to love myself.

With that said, I still want to call home. I can't find the words to express it but I feel as if you all understand. Did I make any sense? If not, then I'm ok with that.

This journey has given me the opportunity to redefine my concept of home. For me, home is my soft place to land, a safe space. I believe that we all need one. What that looks like for each of us is as diverse as we are.

I am in the process of creating that space, both in my heart and in the physical. Each day, I learn a bit more about how to do that and what that looks like. Each person that I have met along the way has given me a "seed." A seed of wisdom, courage, hope, insight or love. I look forward, with joy, to the day that I can take all of those seeds and plant them in my own garden, in my own home.

I'm back on the road today and headed to see a friend in Ohio. I have a feeling that I'm going to need some company for this part of the trip so I'm sure I'll be checking in along the way.

Sending you all Love from the road. Go give someone a call and tell them how grateful you are to have them in your life.

To the Road Trip!

~Robin

August 15, 2012 (Whitestown, IN)

Fellow travelers!

The road has turned me into a rebel: I'm not wearing socks.

Back on the road today and headed to Ohio to stay with a friend and her newborn twins. Baby energy always does my heart good.

To the Road Trip!

~Robin

I had a fresh pair of chucks that I had been saving in the box for a special occasion. While on the road I realized that everyday was a special occasion, so I broke those puppies out.

August 15, 2012 (Chillicothe, OH)

Fellow travelers, safe and sound in Ohio and so grateful to be here.

Think back on your day and bring to mind all the things that made you smile. Send up a thought of gratitude for all the good that came your way.

Today I am grateful for new friends, kindness, clouds, babies and for feeling so loved in this right now moment.

To the Road Trip.

(No exclamation point tonight. There are sweet sleeping twin babies in the next room and I don't want to wake them.)

Rest well all, see you soon.

~Robin

August 16, 2012 (Chillcothe, OH)

Fellow travelers!

Lots of people call me delusional for what I'm doing. I prefer to think of it as living unchained by the confines of a limiting reality.

Same thing.

To reality, whatever the hell that is!

~Robin

August 17, 2012 (Chillicothe, OH)

Fellow travelers!

This morning I woke up and it didn't even feel like real life: Have I really been on a Road Trip for 3 months?

Ok, then, let's get this party started. The basics:

Where are you? Chillicothe, OH

Where are you headed next? You're cute when you ask that.

Now that we've got that out of the way, let's catch up.

Three days. Three days (for the most part) is the longest that I've allowed myself to stay (in good conscience) at any one place along the journey. It doesn't matter how gracious the host is or if they have said that I can stay for as long as I need to. And it also doesn't matter if I actually really do need to stay for a little while. As the second day comes to a close, I start packing.

This morning I had to sit with why that was. What came to me is that feeling as if I am an inconvenience to someone or that my presence is a burden is something that my Spirit is unable to handle right now. There is too much else for my mind to process on this journey. I'm well aware that this is an old belief. With that said I'm still feeling a tad fragile around it.

This morning was my third day in Chillicothe. I get in my car to head to the library and she won't start. C'mon man! I was done. The past couple of weeks have been more of a challenge than usual and this was just the thing needed to push the peaceful road warrior over the edge. After my moment of self-inflicted drama, I picked up the nearest book to see if there was a message in there for me. The message I received was about the power of words and the hold that they can have over our lives. I sat and thought about how that applied in that right then moment.

A flood of emotion came over me. As a child, I remember it being clearly relayed that I was an inconvenience. My presence did not bring joy and light to the people around me. I knew this. As an adult, this is still present for me.

Back to the story.

Here I was in my friends driveway, my car won't start and I choose that moment to read the book "The Four Agreements." Brilliant. Just then, my friend gets home for her lunch break. "If you need some help, my Stepfather used to be a master mechanic, he can help." Say what? Thank you! He was a wise older gentleman but he still knew his trade like the back of his hand. My Zora was up and running in 20 minutes!

That would have been enough of a blessing for me but there was more to come. We went inside to wash our hands and he, his wife and I all began to talk. I shared about my journey and they shared about ones they had taken. We fellowshipped and connected. They offered me life lessons to take on the road. It was a priceless moment that I wouldn't have traded for anything. As we brought our time together to a close, they gave me their number. "Call anytime of day, even if it's midnight. we'll get up."

In that moment, the part of me that always felt unworthy of anyone's time, was soothed. The words that they spoke, healed.

That was my lesson for the day: The words of the past might have shaped who I am in this moment. However, it is the words of Love spoken today that will transform me into who I am to become.

Zora, I'm actually grateful that you didn't start this morning. Tomorrow is a different story. Tomorrow, we ride!

We each touch each other's lives everyday, remember to handle with care.

To the Road Trip!

~Robin

August 18, 2012 (Chillicothe, OH)

Fellow travelers!

Time to get back on the road! I was considering Florida by way of the East coast. Or maybe out West via Colorado and all those states that I can't think of at the moment. If you know of somewhere I should visit, a place that I can stay for a few days or any other helpful tips then let me know. Thanks everyone!

To the Road Trip!

~Robin

August 18, 2012 (St.Louis, MO)

Fellow travelers!

Colorado, via the Midwest, here I come! If you know of anyone along the route (from Ohio to Colorado) then please reach out. I'm not attached to which way I go. I'm really, really, really open to some friendly familiar faces in the Midwest states.

If you've written to me in the past couple of days, I'll get back to you soon. Had challenges finding wifi along the way in Indiana. Near St. Louis now and in search of a place to stay for the evening. Also looking for places near Boulder and Colorado Springs, Colorado for tomorrow. Been a bumpy and emotional day on the road but I've set the intention to have a peaceful and comfortable evening. Thanks for the good vibes, everyone.

To the Road Trip!

Still? Yep, still.

~Robin

August 19, 2012 (Fairview Heights, IL)

Fellow travelers!

GPS says I'm in Fairview Heights, IL. Good to know. Anyone near there? I'm visioning a bed for the night. And cookies, cookies would be nice too.

To cookies!

~Robin

August 19, 2012 (St. Louis, MO)

Fellow travelers! I'm still en route to Colorado and I spent last night in Louisville, Kentucky with the family of one of my good friends.

Today it was all about the cornfields. Seriously. All. Day. They were beautiful! I was tempted to get out and run through one. However, I'm height challenged. That might not have ended well.

At the moment I'm in St. Louis. I am seriously out of my comfort zone in this part of the journey. On the East coast, I knew a familiar face was no more than a couple hours away in any direction.

Out here, it's just me. And the cornfields.

I have around 800 more miles to go, $50 bucks in my pocket and not a clue where I am resting my head tonight. However, as odd as it sounds, I still know, trust and believe that all is well. Why worry, the Universe has my back.

Send up good thoughts for a comfortable and welcoming place for me to stay tonight. Thanks everyone.

Anyone else need a rest? I do. Go on, take all the time you need. It's ok.

Oh yeah, and I did some math. I've driven over 15,000 miles in 3 months. Woah! Ok, bed time for the peaceful road warrior. Goodnight everyone.

To the next 15,000 miles!

~Robin

August 20, 2012 (Fairview Heights, Illinois)

Fellow travelers, a brand new day on the road that is full of possibility! It's 5:30am here in Illinois and I'm waiting to watch the sun come up. A priceless moment.

I receive lots of emails asking why and how I'm doing this. Time for a Road Trip rewind! 3 months ago, due to years of old limiting beliefs and unloving choices, I found myself without a place to live. It happens.

I had two options: allow this to break my Spirit or turn it into an opportunity for healing and an adventure. I went for the adventure, no doubt. I left with $20 to my name, 2 suitcases of clothes, all the books I could fit and a pillow. That was 90 days ago.

For real? For reals.

I've made it this far on faith, trust, friends, family, you all, gratitude, love and kindness. Thank you! This has been an incredible exercise in learning that the Universe really does have me covered. With that said, there have been plenty of days where I've "camped out" in my car. There have also been times where there wasn't enough, in the moment, for a meal or gas for my car. Does that mean that I wasn't provided for that day? Not at all. It was still all good. All good.

I chose to shift my perspective. Being without a warm bed or a hot meal is uncomfortable, but that's it. It made realize how much I have to be grateful for. It also showed me how much I had complained in the past...about nothing.

Today I choose LOVE.
Today I choose gratitude.
Today I choose an open heart.
Today I choose JOY.
Today I choose a willing Spirit.
Thank you, Universe!

Here's the other piece: I have taken a good bit of heat for how I am financing this trip. I can understand why. What I imagine it looks like from the outside is: "Yo, pay me to travel the country!" Gracious, not quite.

The people that have supported me know my heart and care about me. They understand how important this soul journey is to me. Many have even been inspired to take their own leap of faith. I think that's beautiful.

If what I am doing speaks to you, then that's wonderful. However, if you just want to join along for the ride, then that's ok as well. All are welcomed.

Ok folks, time to get on the road. Send up some positive thoughts and good vibes for me. Thanks everyone.

To the Road Trip!

-Robin

August 20, 2012 (Olathe, KS)

Fellow travelers!

I just ran through a cornfield. It was as awesome as I knew it would be.

The cornfield that I ran through in Kansas. If you're near a cornfield, I highly recommend it.

August 20, 2012 (Olathe, KS)

Fellow travelers!

I have enough gas in the tank and energy on reserve to make it to Kansas City or Topeka tonight. Hmmm, I wonder if there is someone for me to meet there? We'll see! Can't wait to see what goodness awaits me! Thanks everyone.

To the Road Trip!

-Robin

August 20, 2012 (Overland Park, KS)

Fellow travelers!

Ok, for real, you all are the BEST! Had no idea where I was staying tonight in Kansas and then one of you lovely people opened your home to me. Thank you Lori! I'm all tuckered out from running through cornfields like I was in a horror movie. I'm going to call it an early night. But tomorrow? Tomorrow is all about Colorado!

But before I go I want to share how amazing it is to me how people (who have no clue how ridiculous and silly I am) open their homes to me with such acceptance and willingness. It never ceases to astound me.

Stop for a minute and take a breath. Take one more, a good deep breath. Just appreciate the moment.

Take care everyone, I'll check in tomorrow.

To the Road Trip!

~Robin

August 21, 2012 (Overland Park, KS)

Fellow travelers, McDonalds pancakes for breakfast? Shucks yeah! I have no idea who this person is.

To pancakes!

~Robin

August 21, 2012 (Overland Park, KS)

"Follow your bliss and the Universe will open doors where there were only walls." ~Joseph Campbell

Fellow travelers!

Good afternoon everyone! No wait, good evening! Aw shucks, who knows. Happy day to you all! There, that works.

Spent the evening in Kansas at the home of a kind and wonderful woman from the page. I really enjoyed our time together. We chatted, shared insights and a-ha moments and drank tea. It was lovely. Thank you, Lori.

Walls are funny things, especially the ones that appear to be real. Right now there seems to be a big ol' wall in front of me and it looks really…real.

Now, I'm not a fan of the word "stuck." I prefer to think of it as perfectly placed in the moment. With that said, I'm currently "perfectly placed" at the Barnes and Noble in Overland Park, KS. The wall the I'm facing looks like thoughts of lack and limitation.

Woah, woah, woah, hold the phone! Lack? Limitation?! I don't think so, yo.

Time for a Road Trip (gentle) reminder:

Dear Robin,

Look at how far you have come, and I'm not just talking about the distance. You have followed your heart even in the face of fear and doubt. You have surrendered to the process and learned how to trust the journey. You have embraced how to be in the moment. You have been provided for, protected, guided and covered. What makes you think that will ever change? All is well, sweet one. All is well. Keep going.

You are so loved,

The Universe

As I was sitting here, that was what I heard. I'm good with that. Thank you, Universe.

So am I really in the Barnes and Noble in Kansas? That would be a yes. What am I in need of? Around $200. $100 for gas to Colorado and the rest for a service call on my car. It's been a long trip for my Zora, she needs some serious love.

What I have learned during this part of the journey: The walls in my life are only real if I choose to believe that they are. No, that's not a wall. That's pure possibility.

To the Road Trip!

~Robin

*The kind host that I had stayed with the night before read my "I'm stuck in the Barnes and Noble" post and invited me back to stay. I was hesitant at first only because I was so eager to keep moving forward in any way that I could, even if that meant going to a new place in the same city. I felt as though if I stopped, then I may not have what was needed within me (determination, faith, trust, etc...) to start again.

August 22, 2012 (Overland Park, KS)

Fellow travelers, my inner child's name is Tallulah Rose. She is the one in charge of this trip, no doubt. We'll get back to her in a minute.

If you read yesterday's post, then you know that the Universe had an encouraging pep talk with me earlier. I was quite grateful. However, I think Tallulah Rose deserves one as well.

Kiddo, this one is from me to you...

Sweet Tallulah,
You absolutely ROCK, baby! You are spunky, full of life and tenacious! I love the way you giggle when someone tells you something is impossible. I love the way you always remember the Truth. You are an expression of pure JOY in all that you do! And Harpo studios? Did you really do that? Outstanding, YES! You knew it was possible all along, I was the one with doubts. Silly me. Wise you. You keep me curious, patient and on my toes. You are kind and good. You are a true teacher. Stay true to YOU! Rock on, little one!
With lots of love,
Robin

Take a moment to write a note of appreciation to yourself. Write it to the "you" that got you to this right now moment. You deserve it, job well done.

To the Road Trip!

~Robin

August 22, 2012 (Common Sense Coalition in Olathe, KS)

Fellow travelers!

Nah, I'm not here. I'm at the library up the street, but I love that a Coalition on Common Sense exists! Common sense (except when it comes to Road Trips) rocks.

To the Road Trip!

~Robin

August 22, 2012 (Overland Park, KS)

Fellow travelers!

I must have some Karma to work out in Kansas. Why do I say that? Because I'm still in Kansas.

Still here while I rest and save up gas money. It's alright. Something tells me that Colorado isn't going anywhere. I'll get there at the precise moment that I'm supposed to, the schedule of the Universe is cool like that.

I'm unclear on what tomorrow holds but this trip has taught me to be ok with that. My plan is to leave Kansas and head to Colorado in the morning. However, that might not be the plan. Going with the flow has brought such peace and gentleness to my life. I don't have to struggle to make anything happen or regret any of my experiences. That's because in my heart, I know that they were all perfectly planned and just what my Spirit required. It's all good. Always and in all ways.

To the Road Trip!

~Robin

August 23, 2012 (Overland Park, KS)

Fellow travelers!

Wooo hooo, just got a job labeling 400 bars of handmade soap with a fellow traveler in the area! You know, I'm really excited. It's something different, it will help me get closer to Colorado AND I get the chance to connect with one of you all! I love spending time with the peoples.

I'll check back in after I finish. I'm sure I'll smell delicious and have super soft skin. I don't need a 9-5, I've got soap!

Let your inner four year old plan one of your activities today. Go out there and have some fun!

To the Road Trip!

~Robin

August 23, 2012 (Overland Park, KS)

Fellow travelers, had such a full day! I made beer soap with the lovely Kenna from Amathia Soapworks and had yummy vegan eats with my host Lori.

In this moment, the peaceful road warrior is feeling tired. I could easily sleep for the next 48 hours. It might just be the road taking a toll. After all, it has been 3 months. I know that all is well, however the minor wonderings and constant wandering has worn me down a bit.

Before this takes a turn into the thunder clouds, let me say this: I'm good and I'm grateful. I know that I am doing what my heart called me to do. Weariness, I can handle. It's all part of the journey.

On that note: Send me some "you can do this!" LOVE, Reiki, good vibes, fairy dust or whatever else you have in your toolboxes! Or banana pudding. Banana pudding is good too.

However, tomorrow is a different story. Tomorrow is all about Colorado! For real. Still unclear on how the next part of this journey is going to unfold. I don't see a way but I know that one can be made.

I think I'm declaring tomorrow Pirate Day on the Road Trip. How 'bout it, who's in?

Goodnight fellow travelers, dream well.

Aaaaarrgh, mate!

To the Road Trip!

~Robin

And on a side note: Someone just told me this trip gave me street cred. Word.

August 25, 2012 (Victoria, KS)

Fellow travelers, remember how I said yesterday was all about Colorado? Turns out, nope. I can almost hear the faint sound of laughter in the ethos each time I attempt to make plans. When will I learn?

This trip has always been about going with the flow. I wouldn't have it any other way.

Today, however, is all about Colorado! I left Kansas 4 hours ago and my GPS has me arriving in Colorado Springs at 11 pm tonight. With all the stops that I make to look at shiny sparkly things, I should be there by 7am tomorrow.

Ok, time to get back on the road! On a totally unrelated yet completely related note, has anyone seen "Beasts of the Southern Wild?" It's a beautiful movie that I think many of you fellow freedom seekers would enjoy.

One of the lines in the movie that had a profound impact on me was this: "the most important thing I can teach you is to take care of things that are sweeter and smaller than yourself."

What a different world this would be if we all did that.

To the Road Trip!

~Robin

August 25, 2012 (En route to Colorado)

Fellow travelers,

My goals for Colorado: 1. Get there.

That works.

A long day on the road. 200 more miles to go until I reach Colorado. As for tonight, it's time to rest. Today was an interesting drive. I must have gone through five different storm systems in a matter of hours. It poured down sheets of rain, got pitch black and then would be sunny and bright 20 minutes later. Through it all, I kept the same pace and continued to move forward. Look at that, kinda sounds like life. I wanted to flip out but that wouldn't have helped much. Instead, I turned up the Jimi Hendrix, put on my game face and kept it movin'.

What I learned today is this: Keep calm even in the midst of "storms", the sun always shines again. Always.

Rest well, everyone.

To the Road Trip!

~Robin

After driving through storms all day, this was what awaited me on the other side.

*A random storm was about as rough as the weather got on the Road Trip. Looking back now, I see what a state of grace I traveled in. As the temperature dropped in the East, I found myself unintentionally heading West. I couldn't have planned it better if I had tried.

August 26, 2012 (Colorado Springs, CO)

Fellow travelers!

Made it to Colorado! I see you all weren't joking about staying hydrated up here. Woah! I feel all tingly and jellyfish like. I'm sitting in the bookstore trying to figure out plans for the night but the thoughts...just...aren't...there.

Ok, pull it together, Robin! Tonight, not a clue. Tomorrow is a different story. I'm going to sit down and see where you all are in the area and start getting in touch so we can connect.

Go on and smile for a minute, just because you can. Thanks for the good thoughts and well wishes.

To the Road Trip!

~Robin

August 27, 2012 (Colorado Springs, CO)

Fellow travelers!

I made an interesting connection last night while waiting in line at the dollar theatre to see "Beasts of the Southern Wild" again. I met Lou Bellamy, the founder of Penumbra Theatre Company. He was in town to direct the play "Fences" by August Wilson at the Denver Center for the Performing Arts. We had a thought provoking conversation about his play and my Road Trip. He gave me his card so I'm going to ask if I can sit in on rehearsals tomorrow. "Road Trip to Freedom", a play by Robin Divine. Yeah, I can dig that. Curious to see how this unfolds.

To New Connections!

~Robin

*I did end up sitting in on rehearsals for Fences. This was yet another experience in which I marveled at how astounding and rich the journey was. As I was chatting with one of the actors between scenes, we began to talk about my travels. He sat for a moment and then said, "I can see your story as a play or a movie one day." Didn't I just say that? I can see it too, I still can.

August 29, 2012 (Colorado Springs, CO)

Fellow travelers!

I didn't intend to be off the grid for the past couple of days but my body and my Spirit let me know that I needed some down time. I don't know if I mentioned it but Colorado has been a part of the

Vision since I began this journey. The past couple weeks, I began to question if I would get here. Things weren't lining up. Forget not lining up, there were seemingly huge roadblocks at every turn. Aw, c'mon Universe! Everything appeared to be saying "quit this foolish journey, it's not for you." In my heart, that didn't feel true.

When I crossed the border into Colorado, I felt such gratitude, pride and joy! I pulled over and wept warm happy tears. I did it. With an open heart and a willing Spirit, I did it. I did it!

I'm still here and spending time with a friend and her family. I'm looking forward to connecting with those of you in the area as well. I'll be in touch.

What I have learned during this part of the journey: Hold the Vision, always. I don't have to know how it's going to unfold. All I have to do is trust. Universe, I trust you. I do.

To everyone that has supported me in any way over the past 4 months, a big THANK YOU! You have made this possible, I am grateful.

Go do something fun, unplanned and not on the "to do" list today. You deserve it.

To the Road Trip!

~Robin

*One major roadblock was money. I had become masterful at working with limited funds, but this experience was different. There were barely any resources flowing in. I searched my thinking to see what had shifted and nothing in particular came to the forefront. However, I knew that something was out of balance.

August 30, 2012 (Colorado Springs, CO)

Fellow travelers,

I think the reason that the past couple of weeks have been so challenging has been because I was focusing on what it would appear that I don't have. In truth, I have all that I need. In my humanness I sometimes forget. And by sometimes I mean often. Bills were coming due and I just wasn't feeling "in the flow" on the Road Trip. Hold the phone, say what?! It's true.

Then the other day I began to make a list. I made a list of every single person that has supported me on this journey. I'm not only talking about those that have made love offerings. I'm also talking about the people that have opened their homes to me, sent me good thoughts, made me a home cooked meal, filled up my gas tank, reached out to their community on my behalf, bought one of my Choose Happiness books, offered me an encouraging word, shared their own stories with me, prayed for me, talked to me when I needed a friend, shared a helpful Road Trip tip with me, met me for tea, shared their time with me, opened their hearts to me and kept me inspired.

To: Pamela, LaKeisha, Marie, Gayle, Edith, Sharon H., Ivan and family, Jamie, Amy M.S. and family, Cathy, Glenn, Lori, Lori-Ann, Alan, Jason, Kimberly, Aurora, Jeanne, Shari, Teena, Kirby, Aimee, Randall, Kathleen, Jane, Jo, Rachel, Maq, Georgianne, Mia, Sharon B., Omayra, Rev.Nancy, Amy C.M., Mrs. Campbell, Jenn, Laura, Stacy, Jennifer and family, Dennis, Doreen, Liz, Kelly S., Karen, Lorna, Robin LJ, Ellen, Ingrid H., Rev. Leandrah, Coach Ade, Chey, Carolyn, Linda, Cindy, Shannon, Michele, Victoria, Barbara, Sharon H., Nicole, Tammy, Diane, Anthony, Carmen and family, David, Carline, Anette, Kenna, Elizabeth, Ola, Ingrid O., Karen, Shani, Kris, Monica, Barnaby, Christian, P.J. and Angie, Jason, Karen B., Coffey, Jen, Chad and Keith, Amy K., Cheryl, Sheila, Michel, Hannamari, Ron, Phillip, North, Nadja, Denise, Kea, Crystal, Jenna, Jared, Wendi, Rhonda, Erika, Lynn, Kelly M., Damon, Stacey, Kate, Colleen, Nat, Tessica, Jen, Shaddai, Janey, Shelby, Ivete, Sue-Ann and L.A.

To you all, from my heart to yours, I say thank you. I appreciate you. I couldn't do this without you.

Sending Love from the Road.

To the Road Trip!

~Robin

August 30, 2012 (Colorado Springs, CO)

Fellow travelers!

To start, I just had tea with the coolest lady from the page. She gave me her tin of Rescue Remedy since I ran out and she stocked me up at the local natural food store. People are awesome. Thank you, Cindy!

Second, I have an updated itinerary: Yellowstone, Grand Canyon, Oregon, California and then Hawaii! That sounds totally doable and reasonable, right?

To the Road Trip!

-Robin

*Soon after I posted this I received a message from a friend. It said "Um, you may want to skip the National Parks...they are having an outbreak of Hantavirus." Really now? Good to know. Catch ya' next time, Yellowstone.

August 30, 2012 (Colorado Springs, CO)

Fellow travelers,

My life is pretty cool...

...and I'm proud of myself for stepping out and living it.

To Life!

-Robin

*There were moments on the road when I truly had to stop and appreciate myself for how far, geographically and emotionally, I had traveled. The same gratitude that I had been showing to others, I finally began to show to myself.

August 31, 2012 (Manitou Springs, CO)

Fellow travelers!

I'm a bit out of sorts today. Just saw a lady walking down the street with a llama. That's completely unrelated to the out of sorts, just wanted to share it. In Manitou Springs on the recommendation of my new friend and in search of fun fruit loopy work/play for the day. According to the sign, Santa's workshop is near by. Maybe I can be an elf.

To the Road Trip!

~Robin

August 31, 2012 (Manitou Springs, CO)

Fellow travelers, today I am grateful for free spring mineral water. Right on time.

To gifts from nature!

~Robin

I may have neglected to mention that at the start of this journey I had a raging case of OCD. I was extremely particular about where I laid my head, where I used the restroom and from where I ate my meals. After four months on the road, I was jumping up and down with genuine excitement at drinking spring water straight out of the ground.

August 31, 2012 (Colorado Springs, CO)

Fellow travelers!

Let's jump right in, how about it? My afternoon started with a fender bender. Yep. Look to the left, look to the right, start to back up and crash! My teacher in this lesson was a teenaged girl. Her day was not going well. Although it was the tiniest of incidents, she was inconsolable. I could relate, been there. I did my best to calm her and remind her that in the big picture, it wasn't that serious. To her, it was the end.

I had a thought in that moment: How often does the Universe do that for me? It sends me signs and reminders that "it's ok" but I'm too wrapped up in my own self-inflicted drama and panic to see them.

Back to the story: After we parted ways, I gave the damage a second look. Forget the dents and paint, my "Choose Happiness" bumper sticker was torn to shreds. That could only mean one thing: it's a sign! Slow down grasshopper. As I told my young friend, it's not that serious.

This was the first in a series of "signs" that caused me to question my journey. Again. "Robin, this is ridiculous. Get some safety and security back. Get a job!" For a moment, I considered it. Then I began to feel a familiar ache in my chest. It was the ache of doing something because I believed I had no other choice. It was the ache of "living" from a place of obligation instead of joy. It was the ache of regret.

But here's the bright side: all that processing, wondering and doubting took place in a matter of moments. Then, they were outta there! In the past I would have stayed in that place for days, possibly weeks. This time around, it was a couple of minutes. I'd say that's progress.

What I learned this afternoon was this: I always have a choice. As long as I do what brings me joy and I share that with others, then I will be provided for. What I offer to others, be it hope, inspiration or encouragement, will always come back to me in the form that I need it. I believe that. I always have a choice and so do you.

Go out there and share your joy! Do what you Love, the world is waiting.

Goodnight from Colorado.

To the Road Trip!

~Robin

September 1, 2012 (Colorado Springs, CO)

Fellow travelers! I'll do my best to keep this short. But again, this is me we're talking about.

Let's do this! My job title at the moment is "student." Each day is a new lesson and my notebooks are filled with them. However, there is one lesson that seems to appear at every destination: Clear complete communication.

To date, I am still not proficient. Work in progress.

The area that it's most present for me is in asking for what I need. The challenge has been in believing that if I ask for what I need, then it means that I don't trust the Universe to provide. I appreciate that perspective, I respect it. However, I believe there is another lesson here for me, for Robin. It's a lesson in learning how to communicate clearly from a place that is authentic, true and transparent.

I trust the Universe with every fiber of my being. With that said, I also believe that the Universe works through each of us.

In this moment, I am in need and would be deeply grateful for your support. If what I am doing speaks to you, you have been encouraged or inspired by a post or you are simply curious to see how the Road Trip unfolds, then please consider sharing any amount that is comfortable for you. Your gifts will go toward fuel for my next destination, healthy meals along the way and safe lodging, in case I am not able to find a host for the night.

If you are unable to at the moment but would still like to support me, then you can always share the page with friends or groups that might take an interest in my journey.

There is something meaningful that will come from this trip, I believe that. With your help, I can continue to move forward and discover what that is. I feel as if this journey is serving a purpose. Not only for me, but for some of you all as well.

Tonight, my heart is content, my mind is calm and I am feeling incredibly grateful. All is well, it always is. Thank you all. Good night from Colorado.

To the Road Trip!

~Robin

Writing posts such as this one was such a challenge for me. What I began to notice was that the level of support that flowed in was always in direct proportion to the heart space in which I was writing from. For instance, if I was feeling doubtful or lacking, then very little opened up to me. However, if I wrote from a place of complete trust and authenticity, then without fail, I would find that I soon had what I needed.

September 4, 2012 (Colorado Springs, CO)

Fellow travelers!

Wrote a song about it. Wanna hear it? Here it go! That has nothing to do with the post, it's just been in my head all day…

Good afternoon everyone! I took a couple of days offline to give myself time to adjust and be present in my current space. I'm still in Colorado but I'm at the home of a new friend. It's another group of kind and welcoming people from the page. Thank you Cindy, MacKenzie and Kimberly!

Each stop along the way offers me a particular lesson. The lesson during this part of the journey has been about stories. Here's the deal about stories: we each have one. There is a reason for the way that each of us thinks, acts and responds to life. There is a story behind it.

Over the past few days, I've had the opportunity to hear a multitude of them and to even share my own. There were some that broke my heart while others were inspiring and wise. There were even a couple that I couldn't wrap my mind around. Fortunately, my understanding of the path of another is not required.

It made me think about my own story:
*What story am I telling to others and what's my intention?
*What story am I telling to myself and is it true?
*Am I sharing my story from a powerful place so that it can support someone else on their own journey, or simply because I can?

The one that made me pause was thinking about the stories I tell the person in the mirror. When I think about the Road Trip, I envision myself traveling to speaking engagements and sharing my message of adventure, trust and willingness. Yes! I see collaborations with people and organizations that have unknowingly encouraged my journey. I can envision it!

And then, I hear it: deafening old stories of doubt. "Now that is hilarious. Who do you think you are? Ha! Who would come see you speak or offer you a publishing deal? What do you have to share that couldn't be written or spoken more eloquently by someone else? You are a riot!"

In the past, that would have halted all progress. Today, not so much. To all the thoughts of doubt, insecurity, and unworthiness, I say this: kick rocks.

I've said this before but sometimes I have to repeat myself. If required, I'll say it again.

With that said, I am Robin. I AM an author, speaker, world traveler and one who enjoys Life. The words that I share are not here to teach, but instead to inspire. My journey serves as a reminder to others that all things are possible. Even that. I offer hope to others because I have experienced what it feels like to have none. That is not what I do, it is who I am.

Road Trip question of the day: Who are you?

It's another beautiful Colorado day and I am off to go stare at the mountains in awe. I have been here for a while but it still astounds me.

Take time today to do something loving and nurturing for yourself. You're wonderful, you deserve it. As for me, I'm going to go treat myself to coconut milk ice cream.

To the Road Trip!

-Robin

After I left my friends house I headed to stay with a fellow traveler from the page. As soon as I pulled into the apartment complex an extreme feeling of heaviness came over me. My host and her neighbor were wonderful. They were engaging, upbeat and lively. The neighborhood itself was much different. There was an energy that I wasn't comfortable with and yet I couldn't put my finger on what it was. I am a big believer that environment can and does have an impact on our emotional health. With that said, I knew that I was going to have to be extremely mindful about keeping my spirit uplifted while I was there. I was well aware of how quickly I could be sucked into the spiral of another depression.

September 5, 2012 (Colorado Springs, CO)

Fellow travelers,

I think I'm ready to plant some roots and hibernate for the Fall and Winter. I want to read by a fireplace, write and drink cocoa. I can still travel, but I'm ready for a bed to call my own.

To home...

~Robin

September 5, 2012 (Colorado Springs, CO)

Fellow travelers,

Cheap wine and friends are good.

~Robin

Alcohol and marijuana were a constant during my time there. They were a daily escape for those that lived there and they became a temporary escape for me. I drank more in my time there than I had in my entire adult life. Marijuana wasn't my preference but I did join in a handful of times. I felt myself shutting down more each day. I had no idea how to keep myself from going down that familiar dark road.

September 5, 2012 (Colorado Springs, CO - 2 hours later)

Fellow travelers,

Update: cheap wine is bad. Friends are still good.

~Robin

September 7, 2012 (Colorado Springs, CO)

Fellow travelers! I'm really (for real) going to do my best to keep this short and sweet. But as usual, zero promises.

Let's do this! I'm still in Colorado Springs and doing my best to enjoy every mountainous minute of it. Those of you that have offered to host me in the CO area, I'm coming! I have a feeling I'll be here for a while (I'll be damned if I didn't call that), I'll be in touch soon.

I have met the most interesting and thought provoking people during this journey. Each time I meet someone, I have the same thought in my head: "Oh yes, I see why our paths have crossed. You are going to share the secrets of the life with me, aren't you? You have some words of wisdom that are going to shift my entire existence and rock my world, right? I knew it!"

I have probably engaged in a hundred conversations over the past months and do you know what I learned? I learned that we are all still learning. Regardless of how intelligent, accomplished, enlightened or profound a person is, there is a high probability that they are on their own journey of understanding.

What I am starting to understand is that we are all teachers and students in each moment. I am also learning that true understanding comes from within. I am open to guidance from mentors and people that inspire me. With that said, the one Truth that I listen to is the one that I hear from my heart.

You know the one: It's not the truth that the world tells you, but it's the Truth that you hear from deep within. The Truth that tells you that you can accomplish a goal even when everything screams that you can't. The Truth that tells you to "look again" when a dream seems impossible. That's your Truth. Your Truth. Trust yourself, you know what to do.

Road Trip question of the day: What's your Truth?

The hosts that I'm staying with are having a community garage sale tomorrow and I'm off to go see if I can lend a hand. Wonder what I can sell? Nah, I'll just give out hugs and magic wands, that's more my style.

To the Road Trip!

~Robin

September 10, 2012 (Colorado Springs, CO)

Fellow travelers, I feel like I've been off Facebook foreva'! It's been 3 days, Robin. Same thing. Still in Colorado enjoying the company and the clouds. I have a couple more stops then I plan to head to Hawaii for my birthday and the Winter months. We'll see how it unfolds, 'cause you know how plans go around these parts. Exactly.

To the Road Trip!

~Robin

September 13, 2012 (Colorado Springs, CO)

Fellow travelers,

I don't know what to do next.

To, I don't even know right now…

~Robin

I was beginning to spin and I knew I was headed into a void. Thoughts of depression were creeping back in. Old self injurious coping mechanisms started to seem "not so awful" again although I never acted on them. I also started to slowly pull back from those around me and also with the people on the page. My fellow travelers attempted to reach out and I found myself unable to reach back.

September 16, 2012 (Colorado Springs, CO)

Fellow travelers!

I desire to go on a shopping spree. In a grocery store.

That's all.

To vegan eats and almond milk!

~Robin

Whole Foods was my Happy Place while I was traveling. Regardless of what city I was in or how much money I did or didn't have, I would find the nearest one and go walk the aisles until I felt like a regular person again. One day while at the local Whole Foods I put up this post. I wasn't expecting anything, I just was sharing a random Road Trip moment. A few minutes later a woman put $100 in my PayPal account and told me to go enjoy. To one of my most encouraging and supportive fellow travelers Pamela, I thank you. That did my spirit well.

September 18, 2012 (Colorado Springs, CO)

Fellow travelers!

I've been in one place for almost 3 weeks, I know where all the Whole Foods, used bookstores and Metaphysical shops are and I can get around town without my GPS. Does that make me a legal resident of Colorado Springs? Nah, I'm not home quite yet.

To the Road Trip!

~Robin

I seriously considered staying in Colorado Springs. It felt as though all progress (Road Trip wise and otherwise) had come to a screeching halt. I began to question if that was a sign that Colorado was where I belonged. In my mind, nothing else made sense as to why I was still there.

September 20, 2012 (Colorado Springs, CO)

Fellow travelers!

California bound tomorrow (hopefully) and I'm going to pull it together and post so that people don't think I fell off a mountain and got eaten by a lion. What kind of a non Road Trip trip is this? It's a Robin Road Trip, enough said.

To getting back on the road!

~Robin

I kept setting the intention to leave Colorado and it never quite happened. Wait, am I back in Kansas? I began to think that maybe just leaving, regardless of funds, was the only way to get myself out of the hole that I was in. It was the most energetically "stuck" that I had felt during the Road Trip.

September 21, 2012 (Colorado Springs, CO)

Fellow travelers!

It's my Mom's birthday! My Mom started a new journey 11 years ago but today I celebrate her time her on this physical plane.

Yo, Happy Birthday Ma! You are loved, appreciated and missed.

And for reals. Tomorrow, I ride. Send up a good thought or two. Goodnight all.

To Moms!

-Robin

September, 22, 2012 (Denver, CO)

Fellow travelers!

Colorado Springs to Los Angeles is 1100 miles. I have enough gas in the tank to go about 50. Am I still confident that I'll get there by Monday? Yup! That's part of the fun of this trip, watching the Universe unfold in reality bending "say what, did that just really happen?!" creative ways. I said all that to say: I'm hanging out in Denver tonight to see the motivational speaker Tama Kieves speak. I know there are connections there but I forget who you are. Will you message me and remind me, please? I could use the company and welcoming smile of a fellow traveler right about now.

To the Road Trip!

-Robin

While at the Tama Kieves book signing she handed out cards each with a different quote. This was mine: "I am willing to leave behind common sense because I don't want a common experience."

I can dig it.

September 23, 2012 (Colorado Springs, CO)

Fellow travelers!

I had planned to be halfway to Los Angeles by now to do some butt kickin' inner work with my mentor in my mind, Mastin Kipp. Instead, I will be selling handmade tie dye shirts and onesies at the Grateful Dead concert at the Red Rocks to raise some Road Trip funds; a creative idea inspired by my new friend and host.. Since I didn't have any of my own hippie attire, my friend let me tie dye her wedding dress to wear. Nice! I'm not givin' up on Los Angeles.

To the Grateful Dead!

~Robin

I had wanted to go to Los Angeles to attend a workshop. And then, the starter in my car stopped. As odd as it sounds, having a legit reason as to why I wasn't moving forward was a relief in a way. Once I knew what the "problem" was then at least I could work towards a solution. Prior to that, I felt as though I was just standing still because I didn't know what needed to be fixed. I raised exactly zero pennies that day but I still enjoyed the experience. My Mother had been a lifelong "Dead Head" and I grew up listening to their music. I felt a connection to her while I was there. It was one of the handful of times that I truly felt her presence on the trip.

September 23, 2012 (Colorado Springs, CO)

Fellow travelers, I want a Mum. Not to do anything for me, just to be there.

To Mums...

~Robin

September 24, 2012 (Colorado Springs, CO)

Fellow travelers, I keep looking for some mega understanding and insight on this Road Trip. But maybe it's not that deep. Maybe it's about doing what makes you happy, finding joy, being kind, learning about love and leaving the world a little brighter. Maybe that's it.

To keeping it simple!

~Robin

September 25, 2012 (Colorado Springs, CO)

Fellow travelers, I have a confession: I am what they call a "people." Being a people means lots of odd things. Here are a handful of them: I do things that I don't quite understand. I feel afraid and confused by life at times. When I don't know what to do, I do nothing. And sometimes, I want to hide and pretend that I'm not me.

That's where I've been the past couple of weeks: hiding. The deeper I climbed into my emotional hiding place, the further I got from Robin's Road Trip to Freedom. I might lose my "Spiritual" card for saying this but I have to tell the truth: Learning to trust in the Universe in each and every moment has worn the Peaceful Road Warrior down.

"Ok Universe, I don't know where my next "insert basic need" is coming from but I know you got this! Oh man, they are going to sell the last few things from my storage that I own at auction? Alrighty then, I know there is a lesson in it! I'm ready to hit the road again but the car won't start. Ok, um, it's all for my good. Right? Right?!"

At some point over the past two weeks, I quietly sat down and unconsciously folded my hands in resignation. "I don't know what you want me to do, Universe. I've done what I can do. I hand it over to you now."

And that, fellow travelers, is where I am.

The basics:

Where are you? I'm still in Colorado Springs, CO at the home of one of you incredibly generous and kind people.

Are you ok? Yes. I'm always ok, even when it doesn't feel like it.

Are you really ok? I am. However, I could use a hug and a heart to heart conversation.

Where to next? Once the car gets fixed (the starter is refusing to start) then Oregon and California. Hawaii has been calling for me as well and I'm ready to answer.

Are you still up for the Road Trip? I am. I choose not to allow a couple of hiccups to keep me from experiencing every ounce of goodness and joy that I can on this trip and in my life.

What I have learned during this part of the journey is this: it's not about what happens, it's about how I choose to respond. If I'm unclear on how to respond in the moment, then stillness is always a beautiful option.

During the past two weeks, I've learned to be still.

If you have been traveling with me for a while then you know that this is not my first, second or even third encounter with this lesson. I am still in the process of understanding how to respond from a place of grace without having to go through the drama of a breakdown. Again, work in progress.

If you'd like to support me with a note of encouragement or an inspiring email then that would be appreciated. I have spent the past couple of days reading over the messages that you all have shared with me. It has made such a difference, thank you for that.

I think that's about it. I'll check in tomorrow, even if it's just to say "I'm here."

I'm grateful to you all for standing beside me.

To the Road Trip!

~Robin

It was during this week that I was notified that the few things that I had left in a storage unit in Virginia were about to auctioned off for non-payment. I mentally scanned what was in there. My heart began to ache as I realized that the one photo album I owned that had belonged to my Mother, was in there. I felt defeated and wanted nothing more than to give up.

September 26, 2012 (Colorado Springs, CO)

Fellow travelers, I officially have a clean slate of material possessions! Time to start fresh.

To releasing the past.

~Robin

I wrote this post moments after having my storage unit sold at a public auction. To this day, the part that still hurts my heart is that someone actually gifted me the money but it came a few hours too late. I was doing my best to find the light in the situation and hold onto hope.

October 1, 2012 (Colorado Springs, CO)

Fellow travelers, did someone say quit? I don't think so. I'm a Goonie at heart and Goonies never say die.

Headed to Oregon one of these days. Maybe. I think. Who knows.

To the Road Trip!

~Robin

October 2, 2012 (Colorado Springs, CO)

Fellow travelers, today is all about gentleness. Anything unlike it can kick rocks.

To walking softly in the world.

~Robin

October 2, 2012 (Colorado Springs, CO)

Fellow travelers, feeling motivated to make some changes today, BOOM! There it is.

I'm out. No more to the Road Trip until I'm actually on the road. That's fair.

~Robin

I have not a clue what I was talking about but something had finally lit a spark under my behind. For that, I was grateful. My time in Colorado began to feel endless. And then in the early morning hours of October 3rd, everything changed.

October 4, 2012 (Colorado Springs, CO)

Fellow travelers, love each other, love each other, love each other. Please.

~Robin

October 5, 2012 (Colorado Springs, CO)

Fellow travelers, not to claim confusion or anything, but I'm feeling confused.

~Robin

October 6, 2012 (Colorado Springs, CO)

"You live like this, sheltered, in a delicate world, and you believe you are living. Then you read a book... or you take a trip... and you discover that you are not living, that you are hibernating. The symptoms of hibernating are easily detectable: first, restlessness. The second symptom (when hibernating becomes dangerous and might degenerate into death): absence of pleasure. That is all. It appears like an innocuous illness. Monotony, boredom, death. Millions live like this (or die like this) without knowing it. They work in offices. They drive a car. They picnic with their families. They raise children. And then some shock treatment takes place, a person, a book, a song, and it awakens them and saves them from death. Some never awaken."
~Anais Inn

Fellow travelers, I'm not sure where to begin. Grab a cuppa tea, this could take me while.

To start, I'm still here with you. The journey continues. it's just a bit idle for the past month. I'm usually in a place for 3-5 days before I feel the pull to continue forward. To date, I have now been in Colorado Springs, with the same kind hearted hosts for 5 weeks.

I tried, however I couldn't understand the reason that I was in that space for such a long time. I didn't have the resources I "needed" to get back on the road and my car was threatening to rebel against this entire idea. In other words, just another day on the Road Trip. That hasn't hindered me in the past so what's the deal now?

Fair question. Let me answer that by saying: I had no clue.

On Wednesday morning I headed upstairs to the apartment of one of the ladies that hosted me when I first got here. I had bounced back and forth between apartments depending on who had space. For the first three weeks, I had been roomies with Kimberly upstairs. Our plans for the day were to make pumpkin chili for 200 people at her job. The thing about plans is that they don't always go as planned. The chili prep wasn't quite complete so we decided to go out and have some fun. Our fun consisted of shopping for children's clothes at Goodwill for the pint sized scarecrows that she was going to make for her office, lunch along with a heartfelt conversation and a makeover at home to end the day. The makeover was for me. She was already a beauty, inside and out.

Kimberly was nurturing and warm and even though she was just 10 years older than me, I felt a gentle mothering energy when I was around her. That was one of the hundreds of reasons that I had grown to love her as a friend over the past weeks.

A couple of other people joined us as the evening went on and at 10pm we called it a night.

Around midnight, there was a crashing sound in the hallway. The neighbor, friend and kind soul that we called Kimberly had fallen down six stairs and had (we later found out) fractured her skull in three places. My host and I rushed out of her apartment and there was an instant feeling of shock and confusion that overwhelmed me. In the midst of our panic, we did our best to help her. It felt like an eternity. Looking back, she was probably at the hospital in less than 5 minutes.

We headed there to be with her, we didn't want her to wake up alone. The hours passed and I felt invisible. They wouldn't tell us anything: we weren't family. They didn't understand: We were her family as well.

On October 3, 2012 at 3am, we learned that Kimberly had passed away.

I'm sorry, what? What?! That's not possible. We're supposed to cook chili tomorrow and you have to show me how to put on eyeliner and you have tiny scarecrows to make!

My soul understood. My fragile human mind, did not.

Kimberly loved and was loved by so many people. With that said, the greater part of her last day was spent with me; a random wayward traveler that she barely knew and yet had opened her heart and her home to. As grateful as I was to have had that time with her, I felt guilt. It "should" have been one of her three boys with her, her Mom, her best friend.

Her Celebration of Life service is tomorrow and I look forward to celebrating the bright light that she was and continues to be.

The picture is from the memorial that her friends and I created on the doorway near where she fell. They are pictures from her Facebook and Pinterest pages that reflect all the things that she loved: her sons, starfish, the Broncos, creativity, the Rock, silliness and volleyball. I send up a prayer and smile each time I pass by it.

Each night before bed, Kimberly said the Ho'oponopono prayer. Today, I say it to her:

Dear Kimberly,
I am sorry.
Please forgive me.
I love you.
Thank you.

Please send up thoughts of peace and comfort for my friend and her sons.

Love to you all.

To the Road Trip. ♥

~Robin

*This experience continues to have an impact on the way I live. Thinking back on my brief connection with Kimberly reminds me that my time here is impermanent. Her life cautions me to truly appreciate the moments that I have been gifted here.

The memorial that we created for our friend on her apartment door.

October 7, 2012 (Colorado Springs, CO)

Fellow travelers, kinda flippin' out but it's all good because I'm beginning to understand. It's about connection! The relationships, friendships and LOVE we share. Without that, what's the point? There ain't none! I'm not connected to anyone at the moment. But I wanna be. Watch out world, I'm coming to a city near you and my heart is wide open.

To Connection!

Oh yeah baby, we're taking this puppy back on the road.

~Robin

October 7, 2012 (Colorado Springs, CO)

Fellow travelers!

Conversation I had with a friend yesterday:

Me: Ugh, I want to go home!
Her: What, you want to create a home for yourself?
Me: YES!
Her: Ok, then do it.

Well when you put it like that. Thanks for the reminder that I actually *can* create that for myself. Often I forget that it's possible.

To Home!

~Robin

*During my time in Colorado I had forgotten what a powerful co-creator of life that I was. To shift my perspective, I began to bring to mind all of the good that I had manifested while on the Road Trip. Choosing to focus on those thoughts instead was the catalyst to get me moving forward again.

October 8, 2012 (Colorado Springs, CO)

Fellow travelers, people often ask me what my most profound lesson has been so far and this is it. The Road Trip has taught me what is truly important in my life and what can take a seat.

To the important things in life!

~Robin

October 8, 2012 (Colorado Springs, CO)

Fellow travelers!

Most of the time I enjoy people watching and gently listening in on conversations of the collective conscience. During a Presidential election year, nope. Respect and love are nowhere to be found. I need some headphones and Disco music, for real.

I'm out!

~Robin

October 8, 2012 (Colorado Springs, CO)

Fellow travelers, I've heard it said that you haven't failed until you've quit trying. True dat! I won't quit if you won't. Deal? Keep making the effort, it's worth it.

To keep on keepin' on!

~Robin

October 9, 2012 (Colorado Springs, CO)

Fellow travelers, one (incredibly big huge) lesson that I have learned during the Road Trip is that Life is (completely totally 100%) all about choices.

Can I control what happens? Nope.
Can I control how I choose to respond to it? You bet I can.

Here's how it's been unfolding for me the past four months:

1. I recognize that I'm not enjoying the journey at the moment. I can either: sigh in resignation while "hoping" something changes OR discontinue doing things that don't make my soul sing while creating my own joy. Word.

2. Things aren't going as I would have planned. I can either: pout in frustration and just accept the self imposed limitation that I have just placed on myself OR declare my intention to the Universe, put in the dedicated effort in and then get to it. That's what I'm talking about!

3. I start feeling sorry for myself about all of the things that did or didn't happen in my life and all the people that did or didn't do them. I can either: blame everyone and then hold a grudge for the rest of my days, foreva'! OR see every person and each experience in my life for the blessing that it is. I can extend gratitude knowing that they did the best that they could in the moment. I can take the lessons that they have gifted to me and allow them to make me better and bolder instead of bitter.

4. I begin to judge the journey of another. I can either: create a world of harshness with my thoughts and my words OR I can choose to see the Love.

5. I start to live in fear about (insert random life event.) I can either: terrify myself with things that haven't even happened OR I can quit it. Instead, I can trust that the Universe has my back.

It's all about the choices. And should I happen to make a choice that doesn't serve my highest and greatest good, then I can always choose again.

This is YOUR life and the choice is always yours.

To Choices!

~Robin

October 9, 2012 (Colorado Springs, CO)

"Once she stopped rushing through life, she was amazed how much more life she had time for." ~Unknown

Quit rushing. That I can do.

To slooooowing down.

~Robin

October 10, 2012 (Colorado Springs, CO)

Fellow travelers! This is probably going to be the most un-Spiritual post ever.

Those of you that have been here for a while know the backstory of the trip. Those of you that are new to the journey, let me catch you up: Four months ago I found myself without a home. As a result, I made the choice to hit the road. Now you're all caught up.

There is more to it, however, those are the basics. Often the details aren't that important.

This is how I envisioned the trip would be: Ah yes, adventure! I'm headed out to the open road and I am about to do this! Concern, worry or struggle? Nah, not for me. This is Robin's Road Trip to Freedom and all of my needs are provided for! But you don't have much money, and what about food and places to sleep? The Universe has it covered. Always and in all ways! Ah-ha moments await me at each destination and I spend my evenings in gratitude writing down the daily lessons I have learned. There is a book somewhere in there. Not just a collection of quotes, a real book. Along the way, I make life changing connections, each one more profound than the last! Wait, what? A publishing house has taken an interest in my journey? Outstanding! They think my voice has a place here and should be shared? Fantastic! Do I want to do speaking engagements, work on a book and inspire others to venture out on their own journey? Yes I do!

This is how the trip has actually unfolded: Ah yes, adventure! Wait, are you sure this is a good idea? No, but I'm still going for it! But why? Quit asking questions, we're going! We're out on the road! And I have no clue where I'm headed. The first day out and I lose a suitcase full of clothes. I end up spending more nights in Hotel Honda than my aching shoulders appreciate. I make frequent stops and shout at the clouds to please show me a sign that I'm on the right path! The few things that I still own are sold in a storage auction and it makes my heart ache. I fall off the grid for weeks at a time because internal chaos and confusion overwhelm me and I feel as if I have nothing to share. Robin? You still there? I've been in the same place for over a month and I have no clue how to get the resources to continue on. Hmmm, what can I sell? Zippo, you don't own anything!

What now? Give up, quit, cry, retreat from life, hide, surrender and wave the white flag?

I could do that. It's always a choice. However, this is me we're talking about. In other words: Not gonna happen. You hear that Universe? Not gonna happen!

Right now, I'm a bit bruised and fragile but I'm still in this. So when you come to see me at one of my book signings or workshops, lean over and whisper to me "you did it." Then I'll know I'm in the presence of a fellow traveler and kindred Spirit. I appreciate you all for being on this journey with me, thank you.

To Staying Open.

~Robin.

October 11, 2012 (Colorado Springs, CO)

Fellow travelers, anyone wanna buy the kiddo lunch? What did you say, am I joking? C'mon man, I don't joke about food. It's one of those days! You can use Paypal and my email. I'll do something kind for someone in return. Who am I kidding, I was gonna do that anyway. Thanks everyone.

To lunch! I hope.

~Robin

And five minutes later, I saw three messages claiming: Done! One of the people sent a note attached: "you are so loved, you are so blessed, you are safe and looked after. Go girl! Show the world what pure love can do. Allowing others to help you along this journey called life develops pure love in us all. I love what you do. I love that through you people are learning pure love!"

October 12, 2012 (Colorado Springs, CO)

Fellow travelers, this feels ridiculous to even write but I can't seem to get enough to eat the past few days. Even when I eat what should be more than enough, it's not enough. I don't know if I'm stress eating, trying to fill some emotional void that I've uncovered or I'm actually just hungry. Aye dios mio.

I was so close to having enough to get the starter on my car fixed... and then I ate almost every cent I had. Aye dios mio, one more time.

I feel as if my purpose in Colorado Springs has been served and my time here is complete. I'm hearing the call to move forward. Truth be told, I'm also hearing the call to find a place to plant some roots. However, that's another post for another time.

I'm taking these physical feelings of emptiness as a sign that my soul is not being fed. I hear you Universe, I'm listening.

Thank you for all the continued Love and support. I couldn't do this without you.

Now let's get back on the road, how about it?

To finding home.

-Robin

October 13, 2012 (Colorado Springs, CO)

Fellow travelers, I write this to the lady last night who pushed through her (very visible) fear and offered me a ride home anyway after my car broke down, thank you. To the hosts that have welcomed my quirky self with open arms and non-judgment for over a month now, thank you. For the people that have bought me a meal, put gas in my car or just loved me over the past four months, thank you. Thank you.

To Kindness.

-Robin

October 14, 2012 (Colorado Springs, CO)

Fellow travelers, check in time! Are you in joy and contentment in this right now moment? If not, then take a deep breath and then take one more. Check in again. As for me, it's all good. Sitting here staring at the mountain peaks, listening to the leaves whisper and feeling quite grateful. Go tell someone you love them, just because you can.

To the moments.

~Robin

Garden of the Gods in Colorado Springs became a place where I often retreated to find quiet and comfort.

October 16, 2012 (Colorado Springs, CO)

Fellow travelers, weepy days for no reason feel unproductive. If I'm gonna cry, then I at least want it to be for a purpose.

To feeling all the feels.

~Robin

*I was without a doubt "feeling all the feels" on this part of the journey. I found myself crying often for what seemed to be no reason at all. In truth though, I was sad. I was sad about losing my friend. I was sad about my things being sold at auction. I was sad about being on a Road Trip to nowhere. And that was ok. This experience taught me that I could feel my feelings (all of them) without being consumed by them as I had in the past.

October 17, 2012 (Colorado Springs, CO)

Fellow travelers, today was about as inspiring as a potato. Tomorrow, however, Operation "Open Road, Oahu and Oprah" gets started! Again.

To potatoes!

~Robin

*I absolutely loved my friends for the continued support and gentle reminders that they offered during the journey. For example, in response to this post, this is what my friend wrote to me: "Then you must have had such an a richly inspired day! There are so many wonderful things that can be done with a potato! And then there are purple potatoes, yellow, wax, Idaho, red, new, fingerlings, roasted, mashed, boiled, fried, baked, riced, oh hashbrowns, and that is only if you are cooking with potatoes. Then there is the art! Oh did you know that if you break a light bulb in the socket you can use a potato to remove the part stuck in the socket? Have a good one!"

October 19, 2012 (Colorado Springs, CO)

Fellow travelers! I had planned to join you last night to post. However, the only thing that I could manage to do yesterday was weep in my oatmeal while watching old episodes of Oprah. Productive? Nope. Soul soothing? Yes indeed.

After a night of rest, I began to understand where the tears were coming from. I was thinking about things. Not conceptual ideas and thoughts but actual things. Books, pictures, keepsakes, jewelry, music and anything else that I feel connected to.

During the past couple of weeks, I have experienced two lessons in "letting go" and attachment.

To start, the few things I still owned were sold in a storage auction. Oops. All totaled, it was probably less than $500 worth of things. But they were my things. My only photo album, a book collection 30 years in the making. Pictures I had collected of what I wanted in my home. My favorite cozy crocheted hat that I looked ridiculous in. Those things that I cherished were probably picked through and discarded without a thought.

A week later, my new friend upstairs passed away in a tragic accident. I had grown accustomed to spending time in her welcoming apartment. I took comfort in knowing that her things would still be there for a little while. I had hoped that maybe her family would let us come and sit on her couch every now and then.

I was shocked when I drove up 48 hours later and saw that her apartment was entirely empty. All the pieces that made her house a home, were gone. All the treasures that she had collected (and would cry over as she shared the story behind it) were gone. Not only were they gone, but they were at the Goodwill.

An entire collection of memories at the goddamn Goodwill. As the thought crossed my mind, my heart ached.

But alas, there is goodness in this. There always is.

Those things are just that, things. My rockin' cd collection and the albums that I had from my Mom were the hippest eva' in life. I might replace them one day but that's not important. What's important is the joy that we had while they were ours for that brief while.

Kimberly wasn't in those boxes that were so quickly boxed up. She is in my heart and in my thoughts. As trite as it sounds, it's true.

It's the memories, the laughter, the joys and the tears that matter. Life is about the things that can't be sold and packed away. Life is about the moments.

With that said, Universe, I am grateful for the things that I do still have. A box of my favorite books, my Moms purse and a handful of photos that I had (thankfully) taken out of my photo album. They're still just things, but sometimes they make the tough moments a bit more bearable.

To the little things that bring comfort.

~Robin

October 20, 2012 (Colorado Springs, CO)

Fellow travelers! This is where I am at the moment.

No regrets - Each was an opportunity for growth. It got me here.
Head held high - You got that right!
Moving on - With grace and gratitude.

Anyone there with me?

To the Road Trip!

~Robin

October 21, 2012 (Colorado Springs, CO)

Fellow travelers! A heads up: this post is going to be a bunch of questions with no answers.

Great. Let's do this!

Question: What is the balance between doing what you Love and being able to make a living?

I've always heard it said that if you do what you love then all of your needs will be provided for. People call it "being in the flow", "Universal Law" or "You get what you give." In other words, if we allow our lives to be ones of Love and service, then that will come back to us.

I love it, I believe it, I'm on it! In the flow, baby!

Hold on grasshopper, not so fast.

If this holds true, then how come so many people that are living from the heart and living a life of service, can't make a living?

During the Road Trip, I have received sincere and caring emails that in short said: "sweet baby Jesus, get a job!" Been there, done that. I have had 20 years worth of unfulfilling jobs that lacked purpose. They have drained my Spirit and extinguished my passion for living. I get one chance at the privilege of being me. Going forward, I choose to spend that time in a more soul satisfying way *while* being of service. But that's me.

As Oprah says, what I know for sure is this: What is true and right for me is not necessarily so for another. What is true and right for another is not necessarily so for me.

Am I refusing to put in the effort and dedication to get to where I want to be? Not at all, I'm here and I'm willing. I'm in this. What I am unwilling to do is further sacrifice and diminish any part of who I am for a paycheck, a person or a sense of security. Done.

I crave independence and a self-sufficient life. I desire to write, inspire, encourage AND prosper! It feels as if there is an inner balance that is not there. It's as if there is a Universal flow that I have not connected with.

I'm not clear where I was going with this post but it's ok. In short: Do what you love. Use your gifts to serve. Protect your heart. Trust the Universe. Live the life that's right for YOU!

It's nice to know I'm not alone in this. Enjoy your time here, it's precious.

To enjoying the ride!

~Robin

October 22, 2012 (Colorado Springs, CO)

Fellow travelers, I think the Road Trip is coming to an end.

That's it.

To what's next.

~Robin

My lack of forward movement continued to make me question if the Road Trip was coming to a close.

With that said, I can't say enough how much I appreciated the support from my fellow travelers along the way. In response to those handful of words, these were the gifts that I received back:

"You've hit a wall somehow, sugar? Well, just think about all the emotions and experiences you've had so far....perhaps just some alone time to digest it all...? It may be difficult sometimes to process everything when the impressions are standing in line so to speak... There IS a solution there for you, a way to make it all flow.... But don't be afraid to say "thank you ma'am" - if the stop-station has indeed arrived. But before you do that.....why don't take some time off....from Facebook, from friends, from the daily routine....to see if there is a flame inside

you that will lead you on, but in a different direction. Either way...I love you and I encourage you, and I am strengthened by you." ~Anette

"Robin. You are source. You are a source of inspiration and a source of light that has gathered light around you so that others may be inspired. Every time I visit your posts I am inspired by those who support you. As for ending the journey, well that is impossible. I believe the journey you took is always an inner journey even though it had an outward appearance. With Winter on the horizon it makes sense that you're feeling the desire to stop and hibernate for a while. We are reflections of nature love. Go within and affirm from your whole being "I AM God connected and God directed." You know exactly what to do." ~KiMani

"Maybe it isn't the end exactly but rather the beginning of something totally new and exciting and beautiful? Perhaps you needed your entire journey thus far to prepare you, heal you, inspire you for what lies ahead? Whether you are putting down roots or on the road, I am still here listening, supporting, and getting inspired. Thank you for that Robin!" ~Victoria

October 22, 2012 (Colorado Springs, CO)

Fellow travelers, I started the day feeling defeated. I wasn't clear if I should move forward and if so, then how I was going to do that. I'm going to head outside for a while and open my heart to some creative inspiration and divine guidance. I'll join you later on.

Take a moment to send up a thought of thanks for all the goodness in your life.

Be well, see you all soon.

~Robin

October 22, 2012 (Colorado Springs, CO)

"I have seen and met Angels wearing the disguise of ordinary people leading ordinary lives."
~ Tracy Chapman

Fellow travelers, thank goodness for Angels disguised as people.

To Angels!

~Robin

October 23, 2012 (Colorado Springs, CO)

Dear Robin,

Do me a favor. Remember this: You are always so much stronger than you think you are. As the Old Hawaiian saying goes" If no can, no can. If can, can." You can do this. Can, can. Thanks so much.

Love,

Me

To gentle reminders.

~Robin

Somedays I simply needed to remind myself that "hey kiddo, you're doing a damn fine job. You got this." This was one of those days.

October 23, 2012 (Colorado Springs, CO)

And wait for it, wait for it….I almost have enough to get my car fixed! Almost there. I…can…do it!

With a grateful heart, I am open and willing to receive all of the goodness that this day has for me. A clear Vision, an inspired idea, a divine connection and a nourishing Vegan lunch. You are so good to me, thank you Universe.

To patience!

~Robin

October 23, 2012 (Colorado Springs, CO)

Fellow travelers, you know what? Life is cool. Even on those days when it feels like an episode of I Love Lucy, it's still cool.

~Robin

There were days on the road that were completely crazy pants. What I learned from that was how to stay in a state of emotional balance regardless of what ridiculousness showed up. To this day, the ability to "maintain in the midst" has proven invaluable to me.

October 23, 2012 (Colorado Springs, CO)

Fellow travelers!

Along the way, I have met some incredible and kind people that have put me up, fed me and just plain ol' loved me. Here's the cool part: many of them were folks I met on the Road Trip! To start there was Amy from the Snow Goose Bed and Breakfast in New York that made soul nourishing meals. Then there was my other friend Amy in Pennsylvania from Happy Inspirational Scrappin! We scrapbooked until midnight! Keith and Chad from Standing Forward were my hosts in Chicago during the Oprah adventure. Had such fun with you guys! Lori from Blissful Awakenings came to my rescue when I had nowhere to stay in Kansas, thank you! While still in Kansas, I had a blast making beer soap with Kendra from Amathia Soapworks!

Oh, and I almost forgot, I was interviewed twice on the radio about the Road Trip: Thank you to Rev. Leandrah from Holistic Truth - Empathic Channel and Brother Ade from Ask Life Coach Ade Radio Show the opportunity! Some people that have consistently kept me inspired along the way have been a fellow traveler on her own journey Elizabeth Anne Hill, Teena from Healthy Happy Home and my friend Pamela. She doesn't have a page, she's just awesome. And finally, the woman that has welcomed my quirky self into her home for over a month, Cindy from Serendipity!

I send a BIG thank you to you all. I could not have done this without you.

To Community!

~Robin

October 24, 2012 (Colorado Springs, CO)

Fellow travelers!

Beyond Meat, which is waaaaay better than chicken, is sold in Hawaii now. I'm taking it as a sign that I must go.

To signs that only have the meaning I give them!

~Robin

*Hawaii seemed to be calling me. I did my Road Trippin' damnedest to look for any sign, including vegan eats, to convince myself that it was where I was meant to be.

October 27, 2012 (Colorado Springs, CO)

Fellow travelers!

Woooo Hoooo, the car is fixed! Thank you to all the kind people that helped to make that possible. I'm leaving tomorrow with or without gas in the car. With gas would be way easier. If the plan goes as planned then I'll be on the road again soon. Looks like it will either be Oregon or California.

It's one of those days where I want to call out "Yo, Mom! Come make it all better!" You ever have those days? On the upside, it's snowing outside and it's beautiful. See you all tomorrow.

West Coast, here I come!

~Robin

Yeah, so I had no plan. All I knew was that the time to go had come.

October 28, 2012 (Colorado Springs, CO)

Fellow travelers!

Time to ride! That's all I have at the moment.

To the Road Trip! Wow, I've missed saying that.

~Robin

I left with barely any gas in the car and got as far as McDonalds in the next town over. I ended up calling the longtime friend that I started my time in Colorado with. She agreed to let me stay for one night. I was relieved and grateful. As I prepared to leave the next morning, I hesitantly asked her if I could borrow $5 for gas. My tank was empty and I wanted to go further than the end of her driveway. I'm still unclear as to why I was cautious when it came to sharing my need with her.

Perhaps it was because she had done so much already and I didn't want it to seem as if I was taking advantage. Or maybe it was because there was a part of the situation that already didn't feel right. In spite of that, I went ahead and asked. I felt as though it was my only option in the moment. I had to leave and that was one way to do it. She seemed to happily oblige without a thought.

A few days later I saw a post from her in my feed. It was not directed towards anyone but it was a very clear complaint. "Have you ever just felt used by someone? Ugh!" I immediately reached out to see what was happening in her world. "You know" she said "I was actually talking about you." Wait, what? I felt as though I had completely missed something. She spent the rest of the conversation trying to explain herself and apologized for not communicating her frustration to me directly. I was taken aback. I didn't know what to say.

However, what I was clear on was that the friendship was over. It wasn't the fact that she didn't want to help me in that way. I get that. No worries, man. I heard "no" plenty of times along the way and I understood. I respected it. They were honoring themselves by speaking their truth in the same way that I was honoring mine by asking. When I told her that the friendship was complete, she didn't understand why. The beauty of that is, she didn't have to. I had grown into my worth during the journey.

I no longer needed others in my life that didn't value and accept me exactly as I was. Her friendship didn't feel loving. And with that, I was out. "Where's the forgiveness?" she kept saying. It was there. What was no longer there was the open door for people to treat me any kind of way. There are too many other people out there that love me. For her lesson, her friendship and for showing up exactly as she did, I am grateful.

October 28, 2012 (Colorado Springs, CO)

Fellow travelers, separation is an illusion. With that said, it sure is a damn good one.

To the Road Trip!

~Robin

October 29, 2012 (Colorado Springs, CO)

"What you are living is a temporary in the moment indicator of the temporary in the moment vibration that you are offering."
~Abraham-Hicks™

Fellow travelers, back on the road tonight. I plan to stop in Utah on the way to Oregon and California. If you have any contacts there that I could stay with for a night, lemme know. Thanks everyone.

To the Road Trip!

~Robin

October 29, 2012 (Colorado Springs, CO)

Fellow travelers, I'm stalling, I don't wanna go. Anyone got any good jokes?

Favorite response: "Want to hear a great joke about paper? Never mind, it's tearable…"

To the Road Trip!

~Robin

*And with that, I was ready to get back on the road. Sometimes a light moment is all you need to keep moving forward.

October 29, 2012 (Somewhere in Wyoming)

Fellow travelers!

You, yeah you. I love you. I don't care if we talk everyday or once a year. I think about you. You're in my thoughts and on my heart. I don't always show it but I care. In my own awkward and fumbling way, I do care. Facebook friends, best friends, family and everyone else, this is for you. Yeah, you. I'm out! Good night peoples.

To the Road Trip!

~Robin

October 30, 2012 (Farr West, UT)

Fellow travelers, emotional butt kicker of a day! 14 more hours to Oregon. It's not that serious, right? Onward and upwards.

To the Road Trip!

~Robin

October 30, 2012 (Rawlins, WY 3:00 am - In response to Hurricane Sandy)

Fellow travelers and East coast peoples,

Doing okay? Take care of each other out there.

Stay safe.

-Robin

October 30, 2012 (Rawlins, WY)

Fellow travelers, looks like I'm going to see my Dad while I'm in California. I haven't seen the dude in 22 years. Wait a sec, was that reason for the trip? C'mon Universe, you could have just told me to call! I would have listened. Maybe. Or not.

To the Road Trip!

-Robin

*At some point on the road the thought to get in touch with my estranged father made its way into my head. I did my damnedest to pretend I hadn't heard it.

October 31, 2012 (Burley, ID)

Fellow travelers, Idaho. Almost there...

-Robin

A stretch of desolate highway in Idaho on Halloween day.

November 1, 2012 (Eugene, OR)

Fellow travelers!

400 miles of creepy bathrooms in Wyoming and McKenzie Pass Mountain (I honestly believed I was going to die on that mountain) both kicked my butt but I made it! Safe and sound in Oregon at the moment. I missed a few connections today, I'm sorry about that. The wifi was limited along the way. I'll catch up tomorrow. Goodnight everyone, rest well.

To the Road Trip!

~Robin

What was so terrifying about McKenzie Pass mountain you ask? A fair question. To start, my car had started pulling hard to the right. Good times. That's all fine when you're on a flat highway. However, Mckenzie Pass was an insanely steep mountain with cliffs, a severely narrow road, sparse lighting and not a guard rail in sight. It was also midnight. Needless to say my heart raced every minute of the two hours that I inched along the cliffside.

November 5, 2012 (Eugene, OR)

Fellow travelers!

Time to get caught up! Last time I posted I was still in Colorado Springs. I set the intention to have my car fixed and be back on the road by Sunday: with or without funds. Sometimes I have to leap and go for it even when I'm not feeling all that confident. This was one of those times. Thanks to friends and their generous support, I got the car fixed and put the rest of what I had in the gas tank. By Monday evening (close enough) I was on the road to Oregon!

As I drove, my heart ached as I thought about you all that were impacted by Hurricane Sandy. I pulled over at a closed McDonalds and watched the storm updates on tv through the window. I couldn't believe the devastation that Mother nature was unfurling. I sent up a prayer for gentleness and calm and got back on the road.

After a 1200 mile trip, I was grateful to have welcoming hosts and a comfortable space waiting for me. That's where I've been for the past four days. Resting, adjusting and getting the knots out of my neck.

Ok, so why the picture? Good question.

That's me, the little one. The other one is Mom. She was good peoples. I shared this picture because that is where I have wanted to go back to recently. It's not that I want to be a kid again, hell to the no. However, I liked who I was in that picture. There was no fear or worry because I knew that I was provided for. I wasn't concerned if other people believed in me because *I* believed in me. I listened to what felt right and true for me and I didn't let anyone convince me otherwise. I was comfortable being me and that was a good place to be.

This Road Trip has shown me how far removed I am from that little one. There has been doubt along the way even though I know I am covered. I am forever thinking about what others think of me. And the kicker: I often trust others more than I trust myself.

Here's the good news, because there's always good news. I can make a new choice. I've said that a hundred times before and that's the point. This journey has been about making a new choice, having a new thought and doing a new thing over and over and over again. It's a moment by moment process. Maybe one day I'll have the "wait, I get it now!" moment and I'll understand it all. Until then, I'll just keep doing my best with each breath that I take. I want to make that little one in the picture proud of me.

To the Road Trip!

~Robin

My Mother and I circa 1980. Mom passed away in 2001. However, I know she was with me every step along the way.

November 6, 2012 (Eugene, OR)

Fellow Travelers!

I'm not who I was before. I'm a continual work in progress and I like who I am becoming. I'm good with that.

To the Road Trip!

~Robin

November 6, 2012 (Eugene, OR)

Fellow travelers, I am ready for a home.

♥ I desire a key to a home that belongs to me.

♥ I see a fridge full of fresh veggies, faux meats and coconut bliss ice cream.

♥ I want to drink almond milk straight out of the box in my pajamas just because I can. (I'll buy a new box if you visit, promise)

♥ I want to sit on the couch and enjoy the quiet anytime I want.

♥ I want to decorate my home with things that bring me comfort and nurture my Spirit.

♥ I want a wall where I can hang up pictures of my Mom.

♥ I see the coziest of bedrooms that welcomes me after a long and productive day.

♥ I picture a writing room where I can...write.

♥ I see a meditation room where I can connect.

♥ I envision a warm and inviting guest room where a weary traveler, perhaps you, can rest.

♥ I imagine myself Happy dancing in gratitude through each room of my home at least once a day.

♥ I see me. I see me experiencing a new level of happiness, joy and contentment that I didn't believe was possible.

I am ready for a home.

That's all well and fine, but how are you going to do that grasshopper? A fair question. Let me answer that by saying: I have no idea. But here's the incredible thing about life: I don't have to know all the answers. I'll release my attachment to how I think it "should" unfold and I'll let the Universe handle the details. I'll set my intention, do what I can in my humanness and then open my arms to receive all that is out there for me.

With all of my heart, I believe that. I do. It's there for you and it's there for me as well. Question is, are we ready, open and willing to receive it? As for me, I'm ready.

How about you?

To the Road Trip!

~Robin

November 7, 2012 (Eugene, OR)

Fellow travelers!

Goodness, it's been a long day. Yesterday, my head was bothering me so much that I slept from sun up to sun down. It was all that I could manage to do. I think the stress of the last 1000 miles caught up with me. When I was out there on the open road, I didn't have time for a breakdown. I didn't allow myself time to stop and rest. All I knew was that I had to get here and I'd deal with the repercussions later. Guess what time it is? It's later, yo.

I made it on Oregon on hope, a prayer and a PayPal debit card that took it's time deducting gas purchases from my account.

On a side note, in my down time I follow a handful of travel blogs. There seems to be such an ease to their journey. How in the ever fresh hell do they do that? Did they cash in their 401k? Are they going off faith? Are they just in the flow of life? But then I realized, this is my Road Trip. It's not going to look or feel like anyone else's and that's ok. The lessons were perfectly planned and placed for me. I'm not completely on board with that yet. I'm at around 72% and getting better with it each day.

Thank you for being here with me.

I'm off to bed, rest well everyone.

To the Road Trip!

~Robin

November 8, 2012 (Eugene, OR)

Fellow travelers!

Time to take some steps towards that home I say I desire to create. As a result, I'm spending the day updating my resume and filling out job applications. First question, "what the hell have you been doing for the past six months?" Yeah, I'll come back to that one...

To the Road Trip!

~Robin

November 8, 2012 (Eugene, OR)

Fellow travelers!

I'm ready to have some fun on this trip. To date, it's been strained. I haven't been able to enjoy my host families or the cities that I'm in because I'm constantly working on where to go next and how to "make" that happen. Universe, I'm ready for a new Road Trip. I desire rich experiences, flexibility and ease. I want to be able to treat my hosts to a meal or enjoy a hotel for a night. It's time for Robin's Road Trip to Freedom to get on the good foot!

Ok, that's all.

To the Road Trip!

~Robin

November 9, 2012 (Eugene, OR)

Fellow travelers, this is for anyone out there that has taken a step on their own journey or has even considered doing so. This is for anyone that has taken that first step by having a new thought, doing a new thing or stretching beyond your comfort zone, I say this to you: job well done. You can do this. Keep going. I say this to myself: job well done. You can do this. Keep going.

To the Road Trip!

~Robin

November 9, 2012 (Eugene, OR)

Fellow travelers! This is me, nice to meet you.

Over the past 6 months, I've had the opportunity to connect with many of you in person. You have shared your stories, your life lessons and your triumphs with me. For that, I am grateful.

With that said, I often feel as if I have not lived up to the expectation of who people think "Choose Happiness" or "Robin the Road Trippin' Gal" is. It's also highly possible that I've made that up in my mind as I have a gift for fiction. Who knows. I'm going with it.

For the most part, this is me. I've cut my hair shorter, it's a tad greyer than before (I've earned it on this trip) and I'm super ok with that. I prefer to listen rather than talk but I'm still engaged. Those times that I do share, my delivery feels awkward and fumbled. I never mean to offend but sometimes I do, please be gentle with me. I often choose silence because it is more comfortable. Even then, I'm still there with you. I mean that, I'm still there.

I don't have inspirational thoughts and ideas flowing out of me at every moment. I'm not a gifted storyteller but the stories are in me. I'm not the courageous free Spirit with the bright, bold energy that I sometimes imagine myself to be. Instead, I'm an observer. I cherish quiet. Solitude and books are friends.

I'm thoughtful, curious and mindful. I make an effort to help and not harm but sometimes I fall short. I have regrets that I've tried to learn from and moments that have broken my heart. I do what I can, like you all, to keep moving forward. I'm a work in progress.

It's possible that one day I'll grow into that rainbow of glitter and sunshine with the beaming presence that I picture in my head. I'm open to that. But for now, I'm me. I'm ok with that too.

Should we have the chance to meet along the way, I'll make you a deal: If there are any expectations on either side, then let's agree to leave them at the door. Let's simply come with open hearts instead. Sounds good to me. How about you?

To the Road Trip!

~Robin

A picture of me from 2011. Back then, that was my happy face.

November 10, 2012 (Eugene, OR)

Dear Universe, I could use a sign right about now. Thanks in advance.

To the Road Trip!

~Robin

November 11, 2012 (Eugene, OR)

Fellow travelers!

Feeling a bit worn down today. Good vibes and hot soup are appreciated. Thanks everyone.

On a side and highly important note: Step into your worth, you're worth it.

To the Road Trip!

~Robin

November 13, 2012 (Eugene, OR)

Fellow travelers, do you know what my biggest Road Trip nemesis has been along the way? Socks. For real, I can't keep up with them for nuthin'! Just had a moment of randomness and wanted you all to share in it with me.

To socks!

~Robin

Later that evening I heard light knock on my door. It was my host and her daughter holding a bag. "We heard you needed socks." I loved my fellow travelers.

November 16, 2012 (Eugene, OR)

Fellow travelers!

I just remembered that next week is Thanksgiving and I haven't made any plans. I'm not looking for an invite, just an observation. I'm not where I wanted to be by this time last year but I'm also not where I was. That's progress, I'll take it.

I wanted to check in and write a post but then I realized that I haven't got a single ridiculous thing to share. However, I've found a solution. In lieu of a post, I'll do a Road Trip Q & A. Let's do this!

Q. Where are you?
A. Physically: Eugene, Oregon. Mentally, Hawaii.

Q. Where to next and when?
A. Geesh, what's with all the questions?! I'm heading to Portland, Oregon to see my cousin and then either Seattle or California. Or anywhere else.

Q. Did you ever get that sock dilemma resolved?
A. Yes! One of my lovely hosts read my distressed sock post and gifted me with a bunch of warm socks. Yay!

Q. Did you know Thanksgiving is next week?
A. I just remembered that last night. Good to know.

Q. Do you have any plans?
A. At the moment, no. However the Universe might. I'm open.

Q. Are you ok with that?
A. I will be.

Q. What in the fresh hell is in the picture, seriously?
A. Vegan turkey deliciousness. Cook me one and we'll be best friends for life.

Q. How's your heart feeling these days?
A. Thanks for asking, it's doing alright. It's been showered with lots of love, vegan food goodness, hugs and rest for the past couple of weeks. All is well.

Q. Are you ready to get back on the road?
A. Ready? Nope. Am I still going to? Yep.

Q. Are you seeing the purpose in the trip?
A. What if the purpose is that there is no purpose and I'm just here to learn how to be in the moment? I know, I answered a question with a question. Be ok with that.

Q. Are you tired?
A. A bit.

Q. Do you feel as if the trip is coming to a close?
A. I do, not quite yet though.

Q. Any Road Trip truths you want to share?
A. Actually, I do have one. Two weeks ago I heard the message to go visit my Dad while I was in California. I haven't seen the man in over 20 years. We barely know each other. When I heard the initial call I felt fear, blame and anger. Then for some reason, it just seemed to melt away with the miles. Totally didn't expect that. This may be the purpose of the whole trip, who knows. Universe, I love the opportunities for growth that you are bringing me. I gratefully (and hopefully gracefully) rise to the occasion. I'll let you know how it goes.

Ok, that's about it! I'm going to head out to a club called The Wandering Goat to meet one of you all from the page and watch you rock it out with your band. The Wandering Goat, I'm totally in love with that name.

Go wrap someone up in a hug just because you can. Take care everyone.

To the Road Trip!

~Robin

Next year, I'll be cooking one of these in my own home.

November 17, 2012 (Eugene, OR)

Fellow travelers!

Thank goodness gracious I can make my own choices. Regardless of how ridiculous they appear, they are mine. Feeling grateful about that.

Thank you for sharing in this random Robin moment.

To the Road Trip!

~Robin

November 18, 2012 (En route to Portland, OR)

Fellow travelers, I'll always strive to be a likable and decent person. However, I'm kinda over the need to be liked. Word.

To being completely ok with who you are in the world.

To you.

~Robin

November 20, 2012 (Portland, OR)

Fellow travelers!

For reals, I've missed you all! I've had the holiday blues and blahs but it's all good. Onward and upwards! I left Eugene, OR a few days ago and headed to Portland to spend Thanksgiving with my Cousin.

I hope there is happiness in your heart today. I hope you are surrounded by people that just want to love up on you. I hope your spirit is filled with Joy and that you feel cared about. Sending Love from Oregon. I'm grateful for you. Happy Thanksgiving everyone! Next year, we celebrate in my home.

To the Road Trip!

~Robin

*Thanksgiving was rough for me. I had been staying in Eugene with the same generous hosts for over two weeks and to be honest, I didn't want to leave. The family was kind, I had my own private space in a separate area of the home and I felt as though they enjoyed me being there. However, as the weeks passed and Thanksgiving approached, I knew that I was overstaying my welcome. With that said there was still a part of me that was secretly hoping they would invite me to share the holiday with them. As the question "what are you doing for Thanksgiving?" came up more with each day, I knew that an invite was not headed towards my nonexistent doorstep. I was hurt. I was back to once again feeling as though I did not belong to anyone or anywhere. What I know now is that was what others do or don't do has nothing to do with me. It's not personal. That was one of the most valuable lessons I learned on the road.

November 21, 2012 (Portland, OR)

Fellow travelers, can we just start with a hug? Thanks for that.

Just a heads up: if you're in the mood for pie, sparkles and inspiring good vibes, then head on over to my Choose Happiness Facebook page. I have Disco grooves for you and everything. But here, here, I just need to be me. It's me over there, but you know what I mean.

I just need to talk.

I've made some choices that have brought me to this right now moment. And in this moment, I am so sad. It's not a case of the Road Trip blues or the holiday blahs. It is a heartbreaking, overwhelming sense of sadness and I have no idea what to do with it. I don't think the cause is from one specific incident. I think it's a lifetime of moments of hurts that were never soothed. And that's part of life, I understand that.

With that said, I'm unclear on how to do better. I don't know what my heart needs or what my spirit is longing for. All I know is that there is an ache that feels almost unbearable. I've done my best to "suck it up, buttercup" and move on but that has not served me well. That's not my path to healing.

So here I am. Where am I? I don't know.

Location wise, I'm in Portland, Oregon with my Cousin. I'm planning to head out in the morning but I'm feeling completely lost on how that's going to happen or where I'm going or how long this trip will go on for. I'm almost certain it will be California but I'm not all that confident in my ability to make the trip. The funds aren't there and more importantly, I'm tired. It's not about the Road Trip, the "tired" is much deeper.

At times I get completely frustrated with myself. Ugh Robin, what in the crud!?! What can I say, it's where I am right now.

I said all that to say, it's ok. I'm talking to myself and anyone else out there that is having an experience of completely clear confusion. Regardless of what it looks like, it's ok. Tell someone what you need, let them listen to you, give them the opportunity to wrap you up in a hug and offer a reminder of reassurance. Whatever you are dealing with in this moment, you don't have to do it alone.

Again, just talking to myself here. I hope you're listening, Robin.

Don't get me wrong, I have had some good times the past couple of weeks. Really, I have! I wasn't able to make it out to the club to hear one of you rock out with your band but I did get to spend some time at the home of one of you incredible people and meet up with another sweet soul for lunch. Jo, you are now an official Road Trip Mama. Thank you. My time with you both meant so much to me.

There are still a few fellow travelers that I want to see while I'm in Oregon. I'm hoping we can plan a Meet-up or two before I leave the state. I'll be in touch, yo.

Thank you all for holding my hand when I needed it. You have kept me going on days when I thought I was done. Love to you all, from my heart to yours.

To the Road Trip!

~Robin

November 22, 2012 (Portland, OR)

Fellow travelers!

Sometimes life is funny in that unfunny kinda way. Even then, it's still kinda funny. Sometimes. And it's still ok. Always. A little tidbit

I learned this evening: This journey is so much more loving when I can remember to laugh.

Oh yeah, and according to the news it appears that the world is coming to an end ten days after my birthday, December 21, 2012. Good to know. Well, I better make it a memorable celebration of another year on this ride! Any ridiculously awesome ideas on what I can do?

To Birthday new beginnings and world endings!

~Robin

November 23, 2012 (Portland, OR)

Fellow travelers!

Today is brighter. Not weather wise, but in terms of my Road Trip emotional health. The past couple of days kinda smacked me in the face. I call unnecessary roughness, Universe!

That's life. We fall down, get sucker punched, feel bruised and then we get back up. On this "free to be me Friday," I am up.

Last night I couldn't sleep for anything and I seriously wanted to. The reason I wasn't able to drift off was because there was this little voice that kept nudging me and I didn't want to listen. You know that voice. That one. What did you say? Nope, didn't hear you. As a result, sleep was not happening. Alright already! What do you want me to do?

I closed my mouth and opened my heart to listen: Find your Dad.

What? Hold on, lemme check. No.

I had heard this same nudging a few weeks ago. However, I shelved the thought and give it zero percent attention. Road Trip tip: not acknowledging a whisper from the Universe does not make it disappear. Good to know.

I have not seen my Father in 20 years. It took me less than 20 seconds to find him on the internet. Damn you Google. I should have done this forever ago. Shoulda, coulda, woulda, buttercup. However,

I am a big believer that everything happens when the time is "right" and not a moment sooner. As a wise friend said, "You are not the same person that you were when you started this trip. The person that you are now is the one that is ready to see him." Thank you Kris. Now that is straight up truth.

I'm in Portland at the moment and the next few stops (one being the town he lives in) are in Southern California. Looks like I have 1000 miles or so ahead of me. It sounds like a long haul but because I'm sensing that I'm nearing the end of this particular journey, it doesn't feel like it. I got this! Right?

Slow down grasshopper, not so fast. At the moment I'm sitting in a library in Portland. I have a Shell card with $15 bucks left on it and no idea where I'm staying tonight. Challenge accepted. A former teacher used to say "how do you eat an elephant? One bite at a time and don't start with the butt." In other words, focus on one thing and don't make it hard on yourself. I can do that.

Focus of the moment: Lunch.

After that: Get to California.

That sounds doable.

While it's true that it takes resources to keep this trip going, that isn't all that is required. Encouraging words, kind comments and loving thoughts also help to not only keep the trip going, but to keep me going as well. If you feel inspired to support me in any of these ways, then that is always welcomed and appreciated.

I'm leaving the library in a minute but I'll check in tonight once I find a place to get settled. I'm curious to see how this will unfold with the Dad. I don't have any plans for what I'll say or do. All I know is that I'm going with an open heart. As another friend said: "Don't over think it." Wise words. Thanks Cindy.

California(ish) bound.

To the Road Trip!

~Robin

November 23, 2012 (En route to California)

Fellow travelers!

You all are wonderful. I came back to my email and found a handful of sweet notes and enough love offerings for a meal and to help get me back on the road. Thank you for that. Going to camp out in hotel Honda tonight but it's all good. Tomorrow is a new day. I welcome the goodness that it brings. Rest well everyone.

To the Road Trip!

~Robin

November 24, 2012 (En route to California)

"It is a revolutionary, world-changing, impact-making act to go at our own pace."
~Nisha Moodley

Fellow travelers, this trip will make a good story to tell to my kids one day.

Indeed it will.

To the Road Trip!

~Robin

November 24, 2012 (En route to California)

Fellow travelers, random Road Trip thought for the day: the feeling of having someone just hold you is so underrated.

That's all.

To Human Connection.

~Robin

November 24, 2012 (En route to California)

Dear sleep,
Let's be friends again.
Love,
Robin

*Insomnia hit me hard this leg of the trip. In response to this post a friend wrote: "Robin, it is said that when you can't sleep, it's because someone, somewhere is thinking or dreaming about you. So you must be on the minds of a lot of people. Be safe out there."

I have no doubt that I was.

November 25, 2012 (En route to California)

Fellow travelers! A late start to the travel day but I'm ok with it. Feeling connected, refreshed, clear and so loved. I'm still on my way to the Redwoods of California and should be there by tonight. Pics have been requested. I'm on it! As always, good traveling vibes are appreciated. Sending love to you all.

To the Road Trip!

~Robin

November 25, 2012 (Tenmile, OR)

Fellow travelers!

Spent last night tucked into the cozy home of two of you wonderful people. I love meeting you all. Thank you Aurora and Rosemary for the love, conversation and inspiration. I was grateful for our time together, more than you all will ever know.

To meeting new friends that are now like family.

~Robin

November 26, 2012 (Ashland, OR)

Fellow travelers!

Detour to Ashland, Oregon tonight then the Redwoods tomorrow in the daylight when I can appreciate them.

And wait, what's that? It's sunshine! Not just non-rain but actual sun shiny sun! Thank you, Oregon.

Next stop, California baby.

To the Road Trip!

~Robin

November 26, 2012 (Cruising along the California coast)

"You don't have to go where you don't want to be to get where you want to be. You can go from where you are to where you want to be."
~ Abraham-Hicks™

Damn straight. And on that note, I'm out.

To the Road Trip!

~Robin

The Pacific Coast Highway on the California coast was one of the most beautiful stretches of the Road Trip

November 26, 2012 (Crescent City, CA)

Fellow travelers!

I was super close to getting my very first Road Trip hotel room with a beautiful California coast view at a ridiculously deep discount. Then my awkward smooth moves stepped in and squashed the vibe. Kiddo, gonna need you to work on your game, I'm just sayin'. Settling in for the night in Hotel Honda near the entrance of the Redwoods. Will head out to explore them in the morning. Yo, I'm in California!

To the Road Trip!

~Robin

Zora the Honda at the Redwoods

*See what had happened was, the handsome desk clerk at the hotel was making it very known that if I wanted a room for a non-monetary exchange then he could make that happen. Wait, say what? Dude, I've been on the road for 6 months and I'm not sure I brushed my teeth today. Are you sure you're talking to me? Turns out he was. And to be honest, I was intrigued. He was attractive, it was nice to feel desired again, I hadn't had sex in more months than I cared to admit and most importantly: I WANTED A BED. What can I say, priorities. I went out to explore the Coast and told him I'd be back later. And I'll be damned if I didn't let my mind run free and started to overthink it. By the time I returned, any heat that had been simmering between us was extinguished by my inability to complete a sentence while maintaining eye contact. Needless to say I spent the night in my car. Again.

November 27, 2012 (Oakland, CA)

Fellow travelers!

Goodness, thought I was in an decent part of town for the night. Yeah, nope. The kiddo is beginning to feel complete with this journey. Going to see a friend in California, connect with my Daddio and then I'm out. I'm d...u...n, done. After that, it's time to create my home. I can hardly wait. What a ride it's been.

What I wouldn't give to be sitting in front of a fire place with a cuppa tea and one of you all right this minute. Your encouragement means the world to me, I truly appreciate it.

To the Road Trip!

~Robin

November 28, 2012 (Yreka, CA)

Fellow travelers!

I got stopped at the California border for a search. I was nervous for a handful of very valid reasons (expired license, lapsed insurance, an ounce of weed from my time in Colorado, etc, etc…) and started mentally scanning my friend list to see who I would use my phone call on. They wanted to know if I had any fruit. Hold on, I damn near passed out over an organic apple? That would be a yes.

To the Road Trip!

~Robin

November 28, 2012 (Willows, CA)

Fellow travelers!

I was mega motivated to get to California so that I could peel off the sweaters and hang out in the warm sunshine. The forecast this morning: torrential and hellacious rain for the next three days. Well played California, well played indeed.

To the Road Trip!

~Robin

November 28, 2012 (Williams, CA)

Fellow travelers, hellacious and torrential rain, my ass! Thanks for this Universe. I gratefully receive it.

~Robin

A welcoming rainbow after a California storm

November 28, 2012 (Williams, CA)

Fellow travelers!

This entire year I thought I was 37. Actually, I'm turning 37. Huh, how about that? I'm ridiculously excited to spend it in California. Two weeks and counting, baby!

On a side note: I'm in search of a comfortable, quiet place for the night. I can travel 200 miles in any direction. Or, if you know of any hotel deals then that would be fantastic-o as well. It's been a long wet drive. I'm ready for a good rest. Thanks everyone.

To the Road Trip!

~ Robin

November 28, 2012 (Sacramento, CA)

Fellow travelers!

The Road Trip is in Sacramento, California! Woah.

I was setting the intention to have a place lined up for this evening but in this moment I still don't. This aching body has been cramped in Hotel Honda for quite a while and I am ready for a bed. Universe, I know you have some perfect plan just waiting for me, right? Ah, I have no doubt. Hold the Vision for me for a peaceful space and a comfortable, warm bed this evening.

One more thing: I'm in California! Oh yeah, baby.

To the Road Trip!

~Robin

After I posted I sat in my car wondering where to head next. Then, this comment popped up: "Not sure if you got my message, but I'd like to gift you a hotel in Sack-a-tomatos tonight. Get in touch if you would like that." As soon as I finished weeping with gratitude and trying to figure out what Sack-a-tomatos was, I messaged him. I told my Road Trip angel that I would indeed like that.

November 28, 2012 (Sacramento, CA)

Fellow travelers!

Wow, look what I got! I am so overwhelmed with goodness right now. I have a beautiful hotel room with a warm bed for the night, a hot shower and all the other creature comforts that I have missed. With all of my heart, thank you. There is a bed gently calling my name. I'll see you all tomorrow. Water conservation be damned! I'm going to take an extra long shower, sleep until my eyes won't close anymore and watch "A Charlie Brown Christmas." A kind man who doesn't even know me gifted the room to me. Brian, you are an Angel. I'm very grateful. Good night my friends.

To the Road Trip!

~Robin

The hotel room that I was gifted for the night by a fellow traveler. And look, even Linus was excited about it!

November 29, 2012 (Oakland, CA)

Fellow travelers!

I am still on a high from last night! Did you miss it? An Angel from the page gifted me a hotel room for the night. Can you believe it?!

For real. Brian, thank you! After more days than I care to count of sleeping in Hotel Honda, I needed it.

I could literally feel the smile on my face as I slept.

I wasn't sure where I was headed this afternoon however I noticed that Napa Valley was close. Hey, I like wine. Napa it is! It turned out to be a beautiful and rainy day in Wine country. I plan to stop again when I head back up North. I feel the need to run through a vineyard and relive my cornfield experience.

For the next few hours, I inched through soggy California traffic. I was intending to go to San Francisco but they wanted 6 dolla bills to cross the toll bridge. Lemme check, no. I'll catch you on the flip flop San Fran. I already spent what monies I had on vegan deliciousness. "Beef" like substance and broccoli to be exact. Completely worth it.

That's where I am now, hanging out in Oakland and waiting to see what unfolds next. The only thing is that Oakland isn't really a "hang out" kinda place according to the fellow travelers. I'm going to take the recommendations of friends and find a town that's more Road Trip friendly for the night. Rest well everyone.

To the Road Trip!

~Robin

Loving Hut Vegan restaurant, thank you for all the soul satisfying Road Trip eats and affordable prices. I completely love you.

November 30, 2012 (Westley, CA)

Fellow travelers!

Oh man, raging Road Trip headache. Send coconut water and a new pair of low top white Chucks, size 6. That should help. Southern California, here I come!

To the Road Trip!

~ Robin

November 30, 2012 (Westley, CA)

Fellow travelers!

Woah, just had a moment. I can't believe I'm doing this trip but I am. I did it. I did it! Check me out, Mom. You raised one decent and tough egg.

To doing what I did not know could be done!

~Robin

November 30, 2012 (Ladera Ranch, CA)

Fellow travelers!

Feeling like a bit of a bad ass at the moment. Drove 400 miles today and I'm almost to Los Angeles. Tucked in safe and sound in Ladera Ranch for the night with cousins. Orange County smells like peppermint and cash. C'mon L.A., let's do this.

As I was cruising down the highway approaching my 10th hour of driving, I had a moment of panic when I realized that I couldn't find my car keys.

As I was driving.

Down the highway.

Sit with that for a minute. And on that note, I'm headed to bed.

To the Road Trip!

~Robin

From Virginia to Los Angeles. Enough said.

December 1, 2012 (Ladera Ranch, CA)

I was once afraid of people saying "who does she think she is?" Now I have the courage to stand and say "this is who I am."
-Oprah Winfrey

Fellow travelers! I made it to Orange County in California. The OC. I am out of my element and I can feel it in how I am showing up. I get the sense that my well worn Honda and tired travel attire stand out. In truth, there isn't one person that has given me a second glance. The judgment is from within.

As I scanned my email before bed, I came across a message from a friend. It was scathing and harsh. Wait, what? Where is this from? I don't understand! What did I do? Or not do?

What I heard in her sharing was that she was not pleased with this journey and how it was unfolding. I, the "unemployed" writer, should not be entitled to travel the country. I shouldn't have the opportunity to have these experiences while she is at home with the kids. She also expressed her discontent with how I seek out support and help from the community.

I had to take a breath.

The initial thought was to defend myself, explain my journey and then lash right back out at her.

"Are you flippin' kidding me! First off, wanna trade? I don't have a home. You come here and I'll go sleep in your bed. I'll have family around and a roof over my head. I won't have to wonder how or if I get to eat everyday. C'mon, let's do this right now!"

That's how I wanted to respond. Instead, I wished her well from an authentic place and released our connection.

I have learned that we call each experience into our lives to support our growth and expansion. I called this in, no doubt. She was reflecting my own thoughts back to me. She put down in writing the feelings of contempt and core beliefs of unworthiness that I held towards Robin.

Core beliefs of unworthiness. Ouch.

As odd as it sounds, this had nothing to do with her. She was a vessel. In each moment, we are all students and teachers for each other.

This was supposed to be a post about my possible visit with my dad that I have not seen in 20 years. I was going to share our story but I can do that now and keep it simple.

The parents met and dated. Turns out he was already married with children. It happens. No heat, no judgment. It was what it was. Instead, I acknowledge that they both made a choice. That was it. After I was born he returned to his family on the other side of the country. Neither side made an effort to truly nurture the relationship. There were handful of awkward visits during my teenage years (the most awful stage in life ever to attempt to build a relationship) but that was it. And here we are.

Which brings me back where I started: unworthiness.

"Wait, what about me? Why do your other children get your attention and care? Are they better than me? Smarter, prettier, more deserving? Tell me what it is, I can change!" Sweet tiny grasshopper, if only you know how little the experience of how he showed up actually had to do with you. Wrap your mind around that for a moment.

And sadly that is what I have continued to ask myself even as an adult. These feelings have served their purpose and I am on the path to being complete with them.

Let's take a moment for a breath. One more.

When caring people question if it bothers me that my dad and I don't connect, I suck my teeth and lie right to their face: Nope. It's easier for me to pretend that I don't care than it is to tell them that my heart hurts.

I feel as though seeing him will offer me a level of healing that I deeply desire. I am unclear if I will have the willingness and courage to go to his door. What I do know is that this is a gift and I am open to receive it.

Universe, please show me how.

I want to end with just who I think I am: I AM lovable, worthy and deserving. I AM a continual work in progress who is a lifelong learner. I AM sensitive, creative and bold. At times, I have questioned if happiness exists for me. I now believe, as Hafiz says, that it calls my name. That's who I am.

I'm going to go find a quiet place to sit and just be. Before I head off into the hills of California, I need vegan pie. Heaps of it. Recommendations are welcomed and appreciated.

That was the longest post ever. I must have needed to share, thanks for listening. It's possible that I'll require a swift and loving kick to move forward, I'll let you know.

To the Road Trip.

~Robin

*The collapse of a yet another friendship caused me to pause and check in. Was it me? Actually yes, because it's about me and not about me all at the same time. We show up in each other's world to teach, grow and heal. Our time together was complete with no heat and no judgement. I was clear on that. I've heard the old adage that people come into our lives for a reason, a season or a lifetime. What my time on the road had taught me was how to discern the difference.

December 1, 2012 (Ladera Ranch, CA)

Fellow travelers!

That last post was a challenge to write but I'm glad that I did. On to lighter and brighter things for a bit, ok? Alrighty then!

As I mentioned earlier, I recently realized (after an entire year) that I am 36, not 37. Good to know.

A friend has generously offered to lend me her address so that I can receive cards. I love cards! You can make a card, send me an encouraging note or put in a painting that your little one created. I welcome it all!

As soon as we figure out the best way to do that, I'll let you know. Remember what it was like when you got a letter at Summer camp? That's what it's like for me on the road. I'm excited about this, thanks everyone!

To upcoming Birthdays!

~Robin

*Little did I know that this short post was about to change my life.

December 1, 2012 (Ladera Ranch, CA)

Fellow travelers!

I got invited to a swanky holiday party this evening. I probably won't fit in at all which means I of course have to go.

To the Road Trip!

~Robin

*I decided to skip the party. Once I realized that I was going to be in a home alone, I quickly passed up a night of shrimp cocktail and awkward conversations in exchange for a few hours of quiet time.

December 2, 2012 (Culver City, CA)

Fellow travelers!

Not feeling very sparkly and shiny today. I think I'll treat myself to a comforting meal and then find a used bookstore to hibernate in. On second thought, I need some love. I'm headed to Agape!

To the Road Trip!

~Robin

Agape International Spiritual Center with Dr. Michael Bernard Beckwith

*Agape became a refuge for me during my time in California. There was so much love there. Agape was the kind of place that wraps you up in a hug as soon as it sees you. The people there take the time to stop, look in your eyes and make you feel as if nothing is more important than that moment with you. It was so soul soothing. It didn't matter where I was in Southern California; if it was a Sunday morning and I wanted to go to Agape, then I went.

December 3, 2012 (Laguna Hills, CA)

Fellow travelers!

I'm headed to see my Dad, I can do this. Send me love.

To the Road Trip!

~Robin

December 3, 2012 (Moreno Valley, CA)

Fellow travelers!

Not the clearest picture but it's all good. I did it. This is my Dad. I'll post tomorrow. Tonight, I just want to sit and reflect. Today I learned that it is the present moment that is important. The past, not so much. Rest well everyone.

To the Road Trip ♥

~Robin

My Dad and I in Moreno Valley, California. I had not seen him over 20 years. For me, that was a moment of completion.

*After I ended the Road Trip we kept in touch. We talked a handful of times and I was happy to have him back in my life. In March of 2015 my Dad passed *away. I attended his funeral and felt grateful to be able to sit alongside my sisters and brother to honor his legacy.*

December 3, 2012 (Between Moreno Valley and Los Angeles)

Fellow travelers!

Woah, I still can't believe that just happened. Thank you Universe, I am grateful. Back on the Road to see Marianne Williamson lecture tonight. Los Angeles, here I come! What a day and it ain't over yet.

To the Road Trip!

~Robin

December 4, 2012 (Santa Barbara, CA)

Fellow travelers!

I needed peaceful vibes after being in the bustling Los Angeles energy last night. After the lecture, I went up to the first Zen Earth Mama I saw and asked her where I should go. "Head to the Mission, honey" she said. Thank you. I'm there.

To the Road Trip!

~Robin

Would I like a wine bottle dressed in a Friars outfit from the Santa Barbara mission gift shop? Why yes, yes I would.

December 4, 2012 (Santa Maria, CA)

Fellow travelers!

Most wonderful comment from my Dad yesterday: "You are your Mother's child. This trip is something she would have done, it was something she wanted to do."

Most awesome comment from his wife: "Did you shrink?"

And on that note…

To the Road Trip!

~Robin

December 4, 2012 (Santa Maria, CA)

Dear Christmas, I see you. You aren't sneaking up on my traveling behind the way Thanksgiving did. I'm taking a proactive approach to the holiday season: One tiny Christmas Tree for the car dashboard coming up.

To Christmas on the Road!

~Robin

December 5, 2012 (Santa Maria, CA)

Fellow travelers!

Just met a sweet, adorable man from Mexico. His advice to me: enjoy life, travel, be happy! Rodrigo, my friend, I like you. On a side note I also checked out his Facebook profile. It said he worked at "not getting locked up again." I can respect that.

To men with goals!

~Robin

December 5, 2012 (Guadalupe, CA)

Fellow travelers!

I'm still here with you. All is well. The past couple of days have required me to stretch beyond my comfort zone even further than I have imagined. I'm in a place of growth, for real though.

This isn't the post about visiting my Dad, I'm still writing that one. This is just a check in to connect and share. What I want to share is this: That thing that you think you can not do, you can do it. You can do it.

Whatever your own personal "Road Trip to Freedom" is, I hope that you choose to travel it. While this trip has not yielded all the answers that I expected, what it has done is far more valuable. For me, it has erased "what if?" and "can I?" from my life.

"What if" has been replaced with: take the chance, trust and believe.

"Can I?" has been replaced with: of course you can, love.

Have you been called to step up into a more expanded way of being in the world? If so, are you choosing to listen? That's the beautiful thing about life, we always have a choice. And in each moment, we have the opportunity to make a new one.

Tonight, I am grateful to be at the home of a friend in Guadalupe, California. She has recently moved in and there is no wifi service for a few more days. I am right where I belong. I am choosing to see that as the chance to rest and read a book. The Law of Divine Compensation by Marianne Williamson is next on my list.

Please, please, please believe in your gifts and abilities and know that any and all things are possible. That thought that just crossed your mind, even that one.

To the Road Trip!

~Robin

December 8, 2012 (Guadalupe, CA)

"Ask yourself this question: Will this matter a year from now?"
~Richard Carlson

Fellow travelers, it's nice to be back here with you. As I said in an earlier post, I've been staying with a friend who just moved into her new home and did not have wifi. Quiet time is priceless. However, now I'm back. Let's do this!

Last time I posted, the Road Trip had taken a major leap forward: I had reconnected with my Dad after more than 20 years. Many of you asked if this was the purpose of the trip: Wait yeah, no. Seeing him could not have been further from my radar. "I don't have time to heal parental wounds from the past, I'm on a Road Trip, damn it!" To which the Universe replied "You're super cute. Think again tiny billy goat."

This past Monday I found myself blankly sitting in my car near his house. I would love to have a courageous tale to share with you about how I walked up to his door with a poised and quiet confidence. In truth, I sat there for an hour crouched down behind the steering wheel.

"Dear Universe, hi. Here's the deal: I can't do this."

The first thought that crossed my mind was how much it was going to seriously suck writing the "I allowed fear to run all over my behind" post.

A second later, his door opened. It was as if the Universe knew that in that moment, I didn't have it in me. It sensed my hesitation but continued to acknowledge my willingness.

Wait, was that him? I couldn't tell. 20 years had worn on his tall frame. His walk was slow but purposed and he rolled an oxygen tank behind him.

He caught my gaze as I walked up:

"Afternoon. Can I help you?"

Ouch. Keep it movin' buttercup, you barely recognized him either.

"It's Robin. Robin Harris? Your kid?" Real smooth, Robin, Robin Harris…

As much as I wanted to jump out of my skin while shrieking in awkwardness, I didn't.

"Robin?" His face softened. "Robin, come in, come in."

I wasn't expecting that response. "Come in, really?"
He gave the same crooked smile that I recognized as my own

"Of course. My home is your home."

And with that, I took a breath.

For the next two hours, we talked without blame, judgment or tension. I tried to find the words to share my Road Trip experience with the analytical Army man that always had a plan. He listened quietly and then said the most beautiful words to me: "You are your Mother's child. This trip is what she would have done. It was what she wanted to do."

Mom, looks like you got your Road Trip. I have no doubt that you were with me each step of this journey. Thank you.

Although our time together was brief, we learned valuable pieces about each other. For instance, our views on life have distance between them. He sees the world as a harsh place to be protected against. I see it as a place of love. He comes from a foundation of separateness. I am in the process of becoming more connected. No right or wrong on either side, simply different.

I'm grateful to have spent time with him as an adult. I'm not the resentful and hurt 16 year old that I once was. My skin is somewhat tougher and my heart is a bit softer.

As I close, I want to be clear on a point: this was not about him. I wasn't in search of his love, approval or validation. This was about me. Over and over again I have been gifted the opportunity to "clean up sh*t" in a relationship and I made the choice, out of fear, not to. He could have told me to go away foreva' and it still would have been a win for me. It was about *my* response in the moment, *my* choice to show up as love and *my* willingness to stand in my fear and still move forward. That, my friends, is what it was all about. I need a breath after that. Feel free to join me.

Job well done, Robin. Well done indeed.

And in response to the quote, will this matter a year from now? Actually, I think that it will. Remember what is important in your life and release the rest with a grateful heart.

To the Road Trip!

~Robin

*As it turns out, the day I went was his Birthday. Well played, Universe. Next year it will be on my calendar.

December 9, 2012 (Guadalupe, CA)

Fellow travelers!

Someone from the Road Trip page just emailed me and said "thank you for having the balls to share your heart." Best. Comment. Ever.

And, and, and...it's my Birthday! Fine, it's in two days. Close enough!

Woooo Hoooo, Road Trip Birthday Party!

Thanks everyone.

~Robin

December 10, 2012 (Guadalupe, CA)

I got a much needed tan today. Winter in Southern California is da' bomb.

Fellow travelers!

Sitting in the California sunshine and feelin' fine! Tomorrow is the kiddos Birthday and I am ridiculously excited for some reason. Wait, there's a reason. I'm here to see it, that's an incredible reason!

If you'd like to send me a card or some other handmade awesomeness, then shoot me an email and I'll get you the mailing address:

It's ok if it's "late", I'll still get it. Things are always right on time! I'm learning that this applies not only to Birthday cards but also to life. It's always right on time.

Stop for a moment and breathe in all the goodness around you.

To the Road Trip!

~Robin

Southern California hummingbird at the home of the kind host that I was staying with.

*I didn't think to look up the medicine of the humming bird until many months after I had finished the Road Trip. When I did, this is what I found: "The hummingbird brings love as no other medicine can. Follow the hummingbird and you will experience a renewal of the magic of living. She symbolizes the enjoyment of life and lightness of being. She invites you to enjoy the sweetness of life and express love more fully in your daily endeavors. This fascinating bird is capable of the most amazing feats despite its small size, such as traveling great distances or being able to fly backwards. Those who have this bird as totem may be encouraged to develop their adaptability and resiliency while keeping a playful and optimistic outlook. Blessed are Hummingbirds and the people who carry their medicine, for they bring color, light and joy to all as well as the understanding that one can be small yet mighty."

That beautiful and tiny bird perfectly embodied what Robin's Road Trip to Freedom was all about.

December 10, 2012 (Guadalupe, CA)

Fellow travelers!

Don't laugh, but I haven't worn shorts since high school and the legs need some serious sunshine. On this day, I buy shorts! This is big for me.

To California tan lines in December!

~Robin

December 10, 2012 (Guadalupe, CA)

Fellow travelers!

As I've shared before I'm staying with a new friend and fellow traveler from the page. She had just moved in to her new home and didn't have any furniture. The next day she bought me a bed. A bed. Here's the thing. She didn't need a bed. She bought it for me. Now that is kindness. I hope that I can one day be even as half as good to someone as people have been to me.

To paying it forward!

~Robin

December 10, 2012 (Guadalupe, CA)

Fellow travelers, I'm learning that people either understand this journey or they don't. Either way is alright by me.

To being ok with what is.

To what is!

~Robin

*I consistently ran across people that wanted to know more about my story. When I shared what I believed to be true about the journey, I found that people either "got it" or they gave me the "I don't get it" blank stare. The people that "got it" didn't have to understand the details of what I was doing or why I was doing it. What they did understand was that I was following my own path. They respected me for listening to my heart even if it didn't make sense to the outside world.

December 11, 2012 (Guadalupe, CA 2:30am)

Fellow travelers!

Ah shucks, look at that smile! Wouldn't have seen that 6 months ago, Road Trip was completely worth it.

On most nights I'm in bed by 9pm. But tonight, I'm wide awake and as slap happy as can be about my Birthday. Just a moment ago it occurred to me why that is. This time last year I was sad. Forget sad, I was depressed. I was living in a place that I didn't want to be in and I didn't want to be a part of this anymore. I felt hopeless. And now, I can smile. I still have my moments where I curse at the clouds in frustration. However, at the end of the day, I smile again. That's progress. I'll take it. Happy Birthday kiddo, you're doing good.

If you had asked me if I thought I would be in Southern California for my Birthday, you would have gotten a resounding: Gimme a sec… nope. And yet, I'm here! How about that? I'm venturing out to go find some inexpensive day o' birth fun. Friends have recommended Venice Beach, Neptunes Net, the tide pools, the Lake Shrine Self Realization Gardens and a certain Starbucks where the celebs hang out. Sounds like a packed day, I'm outta here! The Birthday gal needs a nap.

I was sitting in my car, no idea where I was and only change left in my pockets yet again. I started laughing to myself because even in the midst of all that, I was happy. That was a turning point for me. In that moment I was completely filled with gratitude.

*What stands out for me the most is that when I wrote this post, I was in a place of such contentment. I was not in search of anything more than what I had in that moment. I was not seeking anything outside of myself. Love? Had it. Peace?

It was within. Happiness? It was mine. And the beautiful part is that no person or external circumstance held any control over the light that I felt inside. I believe it was in that moment that I called (even more) Love into my life. I said all that to say: whatever you are calling into your life, BE it. Embody it, embrace it and claim it as already yours. Want for nothing and be ready for it all.

December 11, 2012 (Santa Maria, CA)

Fellow travelers, it's my Birthday! I was headed to Venice Beach to check out the town but didn't quite make it there. I hadn't realized how far it was from where I am. I need a bit more prep time and something in my pockets (besides gum) to make that trip. I'll give it a go next weekend. Instead, I stayed local and visited some of the sights in Santa Maria, California. I gave myself the gift of breathing space for the day.

To Birthdays on the Road!

~Robin

Lake Cachuma in Santa Barbara and Santa Maria Beach in California.

*Remember that post about Birthday cards that I said changed my life? Stay with me, I'm getting there. For this story we have to roll back to 2011 to the never ending Spiritual Life Development program that I was attending. In the course, there were two groups of students that attended, first year and second year students. I was in the second year. The two classes hardly ever crossed paths except for a handful of times when we all congregated in the lunchroom during breaks.

One day while chatting with a friend, I heard the most joyful and infectious laugh from across the room. I turned around to see who it was. I was so overcome by the radiance of the presence before me that I had to sit down. I turned to my friend and with complete sincerity said "I don't know who that is but I already love her." That's right folks, it was woman. Although she was incredibly beautiful, there was something else about her. There was a light that radiated from her. As soon as I saw her, it was as if my heart said "there you are, I've been waiting for you." I had never believed in love at first sight until that moment. I learned (a year later) that she had taken notice of me as well.

But here's the thing: we never spoke. Our classes resumed shortly after that and we went our separate ways. I walked away not even knowing her name. I left the program (again) the following month. I figured that I would never see her again. I chalked it up to a sweet quick connection and went on with my life.

December 12, 2012 (Guadalupe, CA)

Fellow travelers, I'm open to sharing about my life but I'm rarely vulnerable. Note to self: let people in, it's ok.

To Vulnerability.

~Robin

*In response to my Birthday post, I received a Facebook message that read "Hey cutie, I'll send you a card!" Yay, thank you! I looked at the name. KiMani, who is that? Nope, don't know her. I headed over to her page. Wait, we're already friends? I pulled up her profile: a picture of a ball of light. Not helpful. I began to scroll through her pictures and it slowly dawned on me who it was. It was the woman that I was so taken with that I had to sit down. It made sense that we were friends, we had attended the same school. At some point one of us must have taken Facebook up on its' friend suggestion and unknowingly accepted. I started looking back through old Road Trip post comments and there…she…was. She was one of the fellow travelers encouraging me on the journey and I had no idea.

After I closed my mouth, I messaged her back. That was the beginning of daily emails, texts and calls that ran late into the night. I felt like a teenager in love.

It was wonderful. The only part that made me feel slightly raw was that she truly wanted to get to know me. After we covered the basics, she wanted more. She didn't care where I was from, she instead wanted to know about what had broken my heart. What I had done for a living wasn't important to her. She was more interested in what gift I had to offer the world. For ten days straight, those were our conversations.

December 13, 2012 (Guadalupe, CA)

Fellow travelers, I know it's late but is anyone up? Not a post, just needed to chat. Grab a cuppa and join me for a bit if you're in the mood.

Question: what makes you feel connected to someone?

~Robin

*I felt confused and I needed to talk. I didn't understand what was happening. I was falling in love with a person that I had never even had a face to face conversation with and who was 3,000 miles away in New Jersey. I kept trying to make logical sense of a situation that had nothing to do with logic. I was being required to drop into my heart and trust in a way that I had not before on the Road Trip.

December 13, 2012 (Guadalupe, CA)

Fellow travelers, I am so flippin' excited about what's ahead! What's ahead? No idea. But I tell you what, I am excited about it!

To what lies ahead!

~Robin

December 13, 2012 (Guadalupe, CA)

Fellow travelers!

2013 is going to be my classy and sexy year.

On a side note, I came up with a quote last night.

"That's just spit in the river."

In other words, that's small potatoes. It's not that big a deal. Remember what's important. And what isn't. Spit in the river: not important. That's Hallmark material, right there.

To the Road Trip!

~Robin

December 13, 2012 (Guadalupe, CA)

"I do not exist to impress the world. I exist to live in a way that will make me happy." -Richard Bach

Live your life for you.

To you.

~Robin

*The following two posts are in response to the shooting at Sandy Hook Elementary where 20 school children and 6 teachers had their lives taken. There was another shooting in the Portland area soon after.

December 14, 2012 (Guadalupe, CA)

Sending Love to Connecticut and to Portland. Sending Love to anyone whose pain is so deep that they feel the need to inflict it upon another. Sending Love to us all. ♥

~Robin

December 15, 2012 (Guadalupe, CA)

Fellow travelers, what can I say. Last night I searched for words to make sense of it all. At some point, I came to understand that there are no words because it makes no sense.

With that said, this is what I have learned.

This journey has been one "show me what you got" moment after another. It's not from a harsh place. It's more the Universe gently saying "I *see* you. I *know* your strength. I *know* what you're capable of." Show me what you got.

Robin, when life breaks your heart and takes away the things you thought you could not live without, show me what you got.

When you find yourself in uncertain situations and it takes every bit of your being to trust in the Universe, show me what you got.

That moment in which your deepest fears are in your face and you can't hide, show me what you got.

And then yesterday, I heard it again.

"My love, in the midst of all that is, show me what you got."

Show you?! I don't have a shred of faith for you, Universe. I plan to get in bed and weep. That's what I have for you, tears. Leave me alone! My heart aches. I have nothing to give. I can't.

And yet, I knew that was not true.

I had Love.

I had a gentle thought to share. I had a kind word to offer. I had a prayer to send up.

What I also discovered was that I had Love for the entire situation, not just pieces of it. My vision expanded and I was able to see how Love and healing were required on so many levels for all involved.

Change is upon us. I'm unclear what that will look like as it unfolds. However, it's here.

My prayer is that we will come together to take grounded committed steps towards wholeness that are rooted in Love. As Arthur Ashe said: Start where you are. Use what you have. Do what you can.

Let's show this world and our children exactly what we got. It's time.

Peace to you all.

To the Road Trip.

~Robin

I took the picture the night before in front of the Santa Maria City Hall in California.

December 16, 2012 (Guadalupe, CA)

Fellow travelers, do you ever do something that makes no sense but it doesn't matter because some experiences are more important than sense? I knew you all would understand.

I'm about to drive 3 hours because I just need some Agape International Spiritual Center Love on this Sunday. For real.

Do something that soothes your soul this morning. It doesn't need to make sense, it just has to feel right for you.

Love to you all,

~Robin

December 17, 2012 (Guadalupe, CA)

Fellow travelers, sock monkey Christmas tree ornament on my friends tree told me that everything in the world is gonna be ok. Thanks Sock Monkey, I needed to hear that.

To Hope.

~Robin

I was searching for goodness anywhere I could find it. That day it was in a Christmas tree ornament.

December 18, 2012 (Solvang, CA)

Fellow travelers, felt the need to get out and experience the beauty of the California Hills. I stopped for a rest and ended up in the cute Dutch inspired town of Solvang. It was a good day.

To taking it one day at a time.

~Robin

Solvang, CA felt like an entirely different country to me. I felt at peace there.

December 20, 2012 (Guadalupe, CA)

Fellow travelers, wait for it, wait for it...

I have a date! Bring it, 2013.

To the Road Trip!

~Robin

My new sweetie and I were becoming closer. I found great comfort from the recent events in our conversations. During one of our talks we made a "light" date to meet. We agreed that should one of us find ourselves on the other side of the country in the months to come, then we would connect. My first thought: "yeah, that'll happen." As it turns out, our date was closer than either of us could have imagined.

December 21, 2012 (Guadalupe, CA)

Whatever is good for your soul, do that.

Fellow travelers, I'm still here. I am. Between life changing events, Earth endings (12/12/12) and the holidays, there seemed to be a great deal of noise in the Universe. I made the choice not to add to it. Silence is needed at times.

But now, I'm back!

The basics: I am still in Guadalupe, California at the home of one of you incredible people. Thank you, Pamela! I've had time to focus on a project, read and rest.

Now, I'm not sure what to do with myself. But that's another post for another day.

Instead, I want to use this post to reflect back on what I have learned. It'll be short and sweet.

To the questions!

What have you learned about yourself?

I have learned that I'm stronger than I gave myself credit for. I often wondered if my highly sensitive self was equipped to handle life. I now know that I am. I'm going to be ok. I already am.

What have you learned about people?

I have learned that each person is a reflection of one another. The people that I felt challenged by were a call for me to love and search myself more deeply. The ones that I connected with were a reminder to appreciate that good that resides within.

What have you learned about happiness?

I have learned that when it comes to doing what makes me happy, no one else has to understand it, approve of it or accept it.

What have you learned about love?

What I have learned about love is that there is no greater purpose for my being. It is all that I AM.

Take a breath and breathe in this right now moment. Remember what is important.

To the Road Trip!

~Robin

The neighborhood in Guadalupe, CA where I spent my last days on the Road Trip. It was surrounded by cabbage. I affectionately named it: The Cabbage Patch.

December 22, 2012 (Guadalupe, CA)

Fellow travelers, a friend told me to dream BIG. Thank you Paolo! I think that's just what I'll do.

And wait, it's almost Christmas! Ok, that's all.

To the Road Trip!

~Robin

December 23, 2012 (Guadalupe, CA)

Fellow travelers, feeling so incredibly grateful in this right now moment. Just needed to stop for a minute to sit in the gratitude and to share it with you. Thank you all for taking this journey with me.

To the Road Trip!

~Robin

December 24, 2012 (Guadalupe, CA)

Fellow travelers! Happy, happy, joy, joy! Just because. I'm feeling quite fine at the moment, I'm sure it shows. This might not make sense, but after all this time on the road, I feel as if I can breathe again. I don't have a single thing "figured" out, I'm unclear on what's next and I have as much money to my name as I did when I left, $20. Really? Huh. And you know what? I feel absolutely amazing. Ah-mazing! I can breathe again. Now when I affirm "all is well," I feel it in my entire being and I believe it. What a gift.

Speaking of gifts, it's almost Christmas! And again, I am excited *just* because. Woooo Hoooo! I'm not surrounded by family and friends but that's ok. What I do have is the most kind hearted host and you all. And while there are not heaps of gifts under a tree, I am so content. I have been given priceless other gifts on this journey such as encouragement and a sense of community. You couldn't pay me to trade that for a box with a shiny bow on it. Nope.

With that said, I am taking my happy behind to Agape for their Christmas Eve celebration. The lovely woman that is hosting me has to work tonight and I want to be around folks. I want to be around some LOVE! Even if I were alone I'd still be around love, but you know what I mean.

In the picture is the Christmas tree that she bought. The thing that's even more beautiful than the tree is that she bought it for the kiddo. I had posted on my personal page that I wanted a mini tree for my car and she read it. The next day we went out and bought a 6 ft tree and sock monkey ornaments. People are wonderful.

With that, I'm headed to Agape! Man, I love saying that.

I send you all blessings of love and peace from the road. I hope that you are surrounded by people that you love and that love you. May your day be filled with cookies, glitter and hugs from little ones!

Next year, Christmas is at my home. You're all invited.

To the Road Trip!

~Robin

Road Trip Christmas tree 2012. And no Ma'am, there will not be a Road Trip Christmas Tree 2013. I'm ready to celebrate at home.

December 24, 2012 (Culver City, CA)

Fellow travelers!

Tonight I watched Verdine White tear up a church stage like it was an Earth, Wind and Fire Concert at Agape. Best Christmas Eve eva'!

Oh, and thank you all for the Birthday cards! Since I'm currently in California (and they are in Oregon) I haven't seen them yet. As soon as I get back to Oregon, I'll scoop them up. You all are the best, thanks again.

To the Road Trip!

~Robin

December 25, 2012 (Guadalupe, CA)

Fellow travelers, Merry Christmas! For those celebrating other traditions, I wish you Joy! There are various celebrations happening this season and each has their own beliefs. However, at the foundation of them all is the same thing: LOVE.

Let one of the gifts you share with others today be your presence. Be Love and express Love in all the ways that you can. A kind word, a hand to hold or a listening ear can make all the difference.

Wishing you a day filled with laughter, hot cocoa and warm embraces!

Love to you all.

To the Road Trip!

~Robin

December 26, 2012 (Guadalupe, CA)

"I hope you feel things you never felt before. I hope you meet people with a different point of view. I hope you live a life you're proud of. If you find that you're not, I hope you have the strength to start all over again."
- The Curious Case of Benjamin Button.

Fellow travelers, may you always live a life that you're proud of.

To living your fullest possibility.

~Robin

*I was quite enjoying my time in California. I'd spend my days exploring and finding beautiful places to sit and write. I'd spend my evening watching the sun set in the cabbage patch while talking to my love. I didn't know what was ahead for me but I knew that it felt right.

December 28, 2012 (Guadalupe, CA)

"An ounce of practice is worth more than tons of preaching." ~Mahatma Ghandi

Fellow travelers, I've felt a bit quiet lately. Perhaps it's because a New Year is upon us. Or maybe it's because I feel as if the journey is nearing the end. Either way, it has me thinking.

What I know for sure is that I have grown over the past months. However, there are still lessons that I have not embraced. The Road Trip has always had a foundation of love and yet, that is not always how I have shown up.

I recently had two of my past host families reach out to me. Both, with love, expressed similar sentiments. They shared that at points during my visit I was reclusive, sad and withdrawn from the very people that had opened their homes and their hearts to me. I would have paid cash money to deny it and yet I could not. It was true. I considered trying to explain the reasons for my behavior. I quickly came to realize that the reasons were not the issue. The issue became how I was going to respond in the face of this awareness.

Pause for a minute and take a breath, Robin.

At times I have been thoughtless and insensitive with the kind souls that I have crossed paths with. I have disconnected from the community here on numerous occasions. In other words, on this journey I have had moments where I did not live the love that I write.

Please, forgive me.

As I continue on, it is my heartfelt intention to show up as love in each moment. When you all reach out to me, I will reach back. I will honor the community that we have created here. I will connect with you more; even it's simply to say that all is well.

To everyone out there, I see you. You matter to me. With all of my heart, I care.

To the Road Trip.

~ Robin

Christmas lights outside of a Church in Oregon. I am the light of the world. So are you.

December 29, 2012 (Guadalupe, CA)

Fellow travelers!

I just realized that I'm nearish to Los Angeles for New Years. Nice! If it were up to me, I'd be in a three day silent meditation retreat at Joshua Tree. Next time. As for this year, any ideas on what I can do? I'm open for something quiet and subdued or a big ol' Hollywood party! Watcha got? As for now, I'm headed to the sand dunes near where I'm staying. Why? Just 'cause I can.

To the Road Trip!

~Robin

December 30, 2012 (Guadalupe, CA)

Fellow travelers, for me, life often isn't that deep. Do what makes you happy. Love each other, practice the art of non-attachment, keep it light, be kind and enjoy being perfectly imperfect you. All the rest, keep it movin' son. It's not that serious.

To the Road Trip!

~Robin

Day trip to the sand dunes of Guadalupe, CA. 50,000 miles in 7 months. Job well done, Zora the Honda. Job well done indeed. I couldn't have done it without you.

December 31, 2012 (Guadalupe, CA)

"I like to be a free spirit. Some don't like that, but that's the way I am."
~Princess Diana.

I would also add: and that's ok.

Fellow travelers, I'm gotta keep it real: 2012 whupped up on my behind with a fierceness. You saw it in my writing and if you saw me along the way, then I'm sure you saw it in my face. But you know what? 2012 ain't got nuthin' on me. I'm here. I'm standing. I'm good. I made it!

And I could not have made it through this year without you all. Thank you.

I look forward to seeing what 2013 has in store for the Road Trip. All I have to say is: Bring it!

In this new Year...

May we shift from criticism to praise.
May we build individuals into a community.
May we transform judgment to acceptance.
May we alter harsh words to healing thoughts.
May we release all that no longer serves us.
May we embrace all that we have been called to be.

Sending love from California, Happy New Infinite Potential!

To the Road Trip!

~Robin

January 1, 2013 (Guadalupe, CA 12:01am)

Fellow travelers, It feels like 2013 is about to high five me with serious awesomeness.

That's it.

To the Road Trip!

~Robin

January 1, 2013 (Guadalupe, CA Later that morning)

"Either write something worth reading or do something worth writing."
~Benjamin Franklin

Fellow travelers, Happy New Year! Based on how I feel at the moment (like a drunken monkey) you would think that I was out running in the hills of Hollywood last night. Actually, I was at the home of my kind host; reading a book and having a staring contest with Spotty the cat.

You know the kid that gets overly excited about an event and then gets so hyped up before hand that they wear themselves out prior to said event? That's me and 2013. Not only am I excited about

New Year's Day, I'm excited about ALL 365 days of it! Anyone else feel that way?

Good things are on the way for us all, I feel it.

To the Road Trip!

~Robin

January 2, 2013 (Guadalupe, CA)

Fellow travelers!

Healthy is so sexy. There is my very own kitchen, a juicer and a fridge full of fresh greens out there that are waiting for me to get my sh*t together and come on home. For reals Robin, c'mon.

To good clean living!

~Robin

January 3, 2013 (Guadalupe, CA)

Fellow travelers, It feels like it's time for a BIG, bold step! I just wish I knew what it was.

Thought provoking comments, outrageous suggestions and unimaginable ideas are welcomed and appreciated.

To the Road Trip!

~Robin

January 4, 2013 (Guadalupe, CA)

Today feels yummy.

Fellow travelers! 4 days into 2013, are you out there creating, loving and thriving beyond perceived limits? If yes, then outstanding! If not yet, then I'm right there beside you.

And with that I bring you: Confessions from the Road…

It's not that serious. I just like how dramatic it sounded.

Let's do this!

1. To start, it's time to buy a new hat. I'm just sayin'.

2. I'm unclear on what to do next. I don't stare at walls often as I find it counterproductive. With that said, I've been staring at the wall for two days.

3. The thought of continuing to travel makes my eyelashes hurt. On the flip side, the thought of planting roots brings up similar feelings of ache. Alrighty then, that's not helpful.

4. I met someone. No really, I *met* someone. The blend of vulnerability, emotional transparency and surrender has broken my heart completely open…and I am terrified in a way that I don't have words for.

5. I discovered that I like mushrooms.

That last one was a stretch. What can I say, there's just so little left to disclose on this trip.

And that's where I am. Breathing, meditating and staying as present and as freakin' humanly possible. Where will I be in the weeks ahead? I was hoping you would know. I suppose we'll find out together.

The floor is open. Friends, do you have any words of wisdom on love or life to share? Mushroom recipes are welcomed as well.

To the Road Trip!

~Robin

January 5, 2013 (Guadalupe, CA)

Fellow travelers, silence is full of wisdom.

Hush. Listen. Repeat as needed.

To my greatest teacher, quiet.

~Robin

January 6, 2013 (Los Angeles, CA)

Good morning fellow travelers! I am completely in love with the Agape Spiritual Center in Los Angeles. I knew I wanted to attend today but there were thoughts trying to convince me otherwise.

I had missed dinner, my eyes were tired from all day on the computer, I barely had enough gas in the car for the 6 hour roundtrip drive and all I honestly wanted to do was chat on the phone with my new sweetie. To which my heart replied: Whatevs.

I ended up driving in yesterday to stay with a friend that lives near Agape. What a blessing. We talked late into the night and shared a beautiful conversation. For me, it was one of those connections that left me feeling lighter, understood and encouraged. It was as if the Universe gave me a big ol' hug through her words. For that, I am grateful.

I'll be at the 11:00 am service at Agape. If you're attending, then I'd love to connect. Just shout out "Yo, Robin!" and I'll find you.

Today do something that nurtures your Spirit. You deserve it.

To the Road Trip!

~Robin

January 7, 2013 (Guadalupe, CA)

Dear clear and loving thoughts, let's be friends again.

Thanks so much.

~Robin

There were days on the trip when I couldn't think a sane and cohesive thought to save my life. This wasn't one of those days, it was one of those weeks. My blossoming relationship, while beautiful, had me in a haze that I had not yet found my way through.

January 8, 2013 (Guadalupe, CA)

"I needed to be alive more than I needed to be (financially) safe. My joy generated my security, then and now."
~ Tama J. Kieves

Fellow travelers, at the moment it doesn't appear that I have a lot. But man, I'm alive and I feel it.

To the Road Trip!

~Robin

January 9, 2013 (Guadalupe, CA)

Fellow travelers, a short story for you...

An Edward James Olmos doppelgänger kept staring at me in the local convenience store.

EJOD: I think you're my neighbor. I drive the gold El Camino.

Me: Oh yeah, I am!

EJOD: You're the lady that dances out in front of your house.

Me: Yessir, that'd be me!

EJOD: I was watching you one day. I kept wondering what you were on...

What I didn't say but wanted to was: "Life, I'm on life dude!"

To Gold El Caminos!

~Robin

January 10, 2013 (Guadalupe, CA)

Fellow travelers!

Quite a few folks that I'm surrounded by are major life playa's to me. Having major life playa status doesn't mean that their bank accounts are overflowing, although sometimes it results in that. Instead, it's a deeper state of living.

*It's the person that feels the fear but continues to move forward towards their Vision.

*It's the person that listens to all the reasons why it won't work and then creates the one reason why it will.

*It's the person that has the courage to stand on their own in the face of criticism, doubt and judgment.

*It's the person that can't even comprehend the idea of limited thinking.

*It's the person that knows that every "no" is bringing them closer to a "yes."

I've read the stories you share with me. You all are out there. I see you.

I'm not sure who I'm talking to out there, but it's time. Step into the calling of your heart. The world is waiting.

I can't say it enough, it's time.

To the Road Trip!

~Robin

January 11, 2013 (Guadalupe, CA)

I need a hug. Or a nap. Maybe both.

Fellow travelers! Just got a phone call from my sweetie. I'm learning what's important in life. Quality time and undivided attention for those that I love is one of them. The 5 hours of sleep that I missed last night (talking on the phone like a teenager) are making themselves known. As a result, I'm heading to my host home for a nap.

Can you believe that Peaceful Road Warrior met someone? It still doesn't feel real but it sure does feel nice. I'll take it.

Rest well everyone, see you tomorrow.

To the Road Trip!

~Robin

January 12, 2013 (Guadalupe, CA)

Fellow travelers, I'm curious, who inspires you?

To the Road Trip!

~Robin

*A response from a fellow traveler: "Everyday people living everyday lives who struggle and smile the whole while. I see inspiration from an old lady watching her grandchildren play on the beach smiling the whole while. A dad changing his tire with his child looking on talking and smiling the whole while. A shop assistant chasing someone down to give back their change smiling the whole while. There is inspiration in the smallest gesture right through to the wise guru with great things to say."

January 12, 2013 (Guadalupe, CA)

"You should sit in meditation for 20 minutes each day. Unless you're too busy; then you should sit for an hour."
~ Old Zen adage

Fellow travelers! I was searching for a quote about meditation and this came in my news feed a minute later. Perfection.

Let me get right to it: I'm ready to have a new experience in life. I'm not just talking about creating a home. I'm also talking about creating the feelings that come with it: comfort, security and a sense of peace. Because in truth, it's not about the home. I've lived in plenty of spaces where those feelings did not exist.

The first step is to get clear on what I desire: what does it look like, what do I hear, who is there with me, what scents are in the air, how does my heart feel when I'm there?

Once I'm clear on the Vision, I go deeper: what loving and committed choices am I willing to make in order to create that experience? This question requires that I tell the entire truth. All of it. Instead of it being a choice that *sounds* good, it has to be one that I am honestly going to take action towards.

And that is where I am. I have very few answers at the moment. However, what I have learned about answers is that they always reside within.

I plan to spend the afternoon in meditation. My mind is clear and my heart is open.

A friend recently shared a thought that spoke to me. She said "Praying and meditating is like plugging into the Universe and saying: let's do this."

I'm all about that. Universe, let's do this.

Take time to focus on you today, you're worth it.

To the Road Trip!

-Robin

In response to the journey, a fellow traveler and new friend that I had met along the way posted this: "Boys and Girls, I want to be very clear about one thing. 'Following your dream' is an awesome catch phrase and has a pretty awesome ring to it. But listen. Listen. There's nothing easy about it. Nothing worth having, as they say, is simply given to you. A friend of mine knows - as a few of you do - there is always a price to pay. It's not at all about being easy, affordable, explainable or justifiable but I guarantee, it's worth it. What makes you come alive? Go and do that. Because that's what the world needs, is people who have come alive."

January 13, 2013 (Guadalupe, CA)

Fellow travelers, I love when people believe in me. It's not required, but man, it sure is nice. On a side note, my friend just told me I had swagger. I'll take it.

To Road Trip Swagger!

-Robin

January 14, 2013 (Guadalupe, CA)

Fellow travelers, I am ridiculously excited about the day! Wisest words of wisdom I received about the my upcoming adventure: no expectations. I can do that.

Wahooooo!

I mean, uh, to the Road Trip!

-Robin

The "light tentative date" I had with my new love unfolded more quickly than I had expected. As the Universe would have it, business was bringing her to

California in the coming weeks. On January 14th, I drove to Long Beach, CA where we spent 4 days with each other. I knew from our first moments that I had found the one. As we said our goodbyes on the last day, I was crystal clear that being on opposite ends of the country was not what I wanted. I knew without a doubt that I wanted to head to New Jersey.

January 17, 2013 (Long Beach, CA)

Fellow travelers!

I see, this is what having fun with life feels like. I like! Took a handful of days away to enjoy the moments. For inquiring minds, it was lovely. I'm happy and grateful.

Sitting alone in the hotel room right after I had put my new sweetie back on a plane to New Jersey. See that face? Oh yeah, I was in love.

January 18, 2013 (Guadalupe, CA)

Fellow travelers!

I'm super grateful that I'm past the age when my phone privileges can be revoked.

To late night chats and new love!

~Robin

January 19, 2013 (Guadalupe, CA)

Fellow travelers! Sitting outside in the California sunshine and this is what I see: Three little ones under the age of 5 are riding back and forth on scooters and big wheels. One of them just rode up right in front of me. showed me his muscles and said he was getting stronger everyday. Then he sped off with an "adios amigo!" For me, life is about moments like these.

These are your moments, enjoy them.

To the Road Trip!

~Robin

January 20, 2013 (Guadalupe, CA)

Fellow travelers, logical thinking is overrated. Life is short. Right now I'm about the Love.

To Love!

~Robin

*I could not believe that I was seriously contemplating moving across the country. It was beyond unreasonable, completely illogical and yet I knew I had to do it. My new love was having similar thoughts on her side. Where I was going to live was a daily conversation. We couldn't live together…could we? We had spent **less than a week** together. Neither one of us could wrap our minds around what was happening. It made no sense. In spite of the clear confusion of the entire situation, we soon made the choice to say "yes" to this new adventure and start a life together. And with that, I was headed to New Jersey.*

January 22, 2013 (Guadalupe, CA)

"Don't tell me how wonderful things will be . . . some day.
Show me you can risk being completely at peace,
truly okay with the way things are right now in this moment,
and again in the next and the next and the next. . ."
~ "The Dance" by Oriah Mountain Dreamer

Fellow travelers, I'm still here! At least, there's a strong possibility that I am. I'm a bit in the clouds at the moment but I'll attempt to make sense. No promises.

Here is what I have learned about this process called life: I trust it, I rarely understand it and I often overthink it.

Aye, dios mio.

Road Trip A-ha moment #472: My thinking is overrated.

Please don't misunderstand. I am *all* for conscious and introspective thoughts; all the rest can take a seat.

Here is a handful of the repetitive commentary that runs through my head on the daily:

I don't get it.
Wait, what happened here?
Did I really just do that? Yes, yes you did.
Am I really about to do this? Yes, yes you are.
Robin, what is your issue, chicklet?
This makes no sense.
French fries for breakfast, yes?
Well now, that was a bad idea.
I completely shoulda gone for it!
I wonder what will happen?
Did you learn anything last time? That would be a no.
Hot damn it all to hell, let's go for it!
For real, I can't with you.

And so on and so on...

That french fry question is a fair one. All the rest, nah man.

Here's the deal with this entire list: Zero percent of it supports me in living in this right now moment. It's also filled to the brim with judgment, did you catch that? What this constant questioning does is keep me tied to the past and nervous about the future. It requires me to make fresh choices based on old information. It makes experiences "good" or "bad" when in reality, they just are. And the kicker, it feeds me the heaping untruth that right where I am, and *exactly* as I am, is not pure perfection.

Lies, all lies! Sit down dammit.

I could spend the rest of my time here judging who I am, living in a box and sticking labels on my forehead. As for me, I'd prefer to live and feel alive. And not just live, but live from a place of love. What that looks like for me is that I am in the moment at *all* times. Instead of reflecting on what "did" or "could" happen, I stay present and listen to the guidance from my heart. We each have that within us. The question becomes, do we have the courage to listen?

In this moment I am making the choice to listen. And with that, I am headed to New Jersey, baby!

I know what you're thinking, "isn't the East coast where you started from?" Technically yes, yes it is. However, I have connected with someone and fallen completely in love. Currently I am in California and they are in New Jersey. With that said, 3000 miles apart does not feel good to any part of my being.

If you all are anything like my friends, then you probably have similar questions:

*Isn't this quick? Time isn't real.

*What if it doesn't work out? What if it *does*. Besides, that's all perspective but I get it. If not, then I'll remember the moments we shared with gratitude and zero regret.

*When do you leave? Soonish or sooner.

*Do you have a plan? You're so cute. Define the word "plan"…

*Robin, questions and answers with you aren't worth spit, are you aware of that? Completely. Be ok with that.

Fellow travelers, I am about to traverse this vast country of ours once again. I'd love for you to join me. Just like I posted many months ago, I could use the company. There's a seat just for you.

I have no idea how this will unfold or where the resources will come from. Luckily, my knowing is not required.

I am completely overjoyed about the day that I will come here and share that I am moving into my new home. I'm still in the moment. And in this moment, I'm also holding the Vision. Always hold the Vision.

Yo, let's do this.

To the next chapter of Road Trip!

~Robin

I had decided to head to Jersey. What I hadn't done was told my fellow travelers that the person that had captured my heart was a woman. In truth, in spite of all the unconditioned love I had been shown by them, I still feared being judged.

January 22, 2013 (Guadalupe, CA)

That last post was super long. I'll condense it for you. Here goes: Do what makes YOU happy.

That was about it.

These are your moments, enjoy them!

To the Road Trip!

~Robin

January 23, 2013 (Guadalupe, CA)

"At first glance it may appear too hard. Look again. Always look again."
~Mary Anne Radmacher

Fellow travelers, whatever it is for you, always look again.

To the Road Trip!

~Robin

January 24, 2013 (Guadalupe, CA)

Fellow travelers!

Often, all I have to do is show up, be willing and the Universe handles the rest. A sage friend shared that with me and it's true. I'm watching that happen now. Loving every minute of it.

On a side note: I'm going to miss California sunsets in the cabbage patch.

To the Cabbage Patch!

~Robin

One of my last nights in Guadalupe, CA.

January 25, 2013 (Guadalupe, CA)

Fellow travelers, I just got super excited about getting back on the road soon for another 3000 miles!

Planning this trip home is already unfolding with way more ease and grace than last time. I have an offer for AAA and possible gifts of hotel stays along the way. Feeling grateful and filled with love. Thanks everyone.

See you soon.

To the Road Trip!

~Robin

*As it turns out, everything I thought I had planned fell through. There was no AAA and no hotel. It happens. Oddly enough, I wasn't deterred. The pull to go forward was greater than anything that could show up on my path over the next 3,000 miles.

January 26, 2013 (Guadalupe, CA)

"We decided that, regardless of external circumstances, we wanted to have a good time in our relationship."
~Katie and Gay Hendricks

Dear fear,
Please kiss my behind. Thank you kindly.
Love,
Robin

*I don't know what was happening with my love in New Jersey, but in California I was feeling the fear.

January 26, 2013 (Guadalupe, CA)

Fellow travelers, holding in the forefront of my mind that one day I will cease to exist in this form makes me want to live each moment like nobody's business. I have a 3000 mile trip home to plan. I'm on it.

To Home!

~Robin

January 27, 2013 (Guadalupe, CA)

Ha! New Jersey. 3,030 miles. I'm hilarious. I appreciate you all for supporting my ridiculousness.

Los Angeles, California to Albuquerque, New Mexico
Albuquerque, New Mexico to New Orleans, Louisiana
New Orleans, Louisiana to Charlotte, North Carolina
Charlotte, North Carolina to Montclair, New Jersey

That sounds doable. Good lord, how I do love you Robin. I leave within the week. If you are along the route and want to grab a cuppa tea while I'm there, lemme know. Good traveling vibes are appreciated. Thanks all. You ready? I am.

To the Road Trip!

~Robin

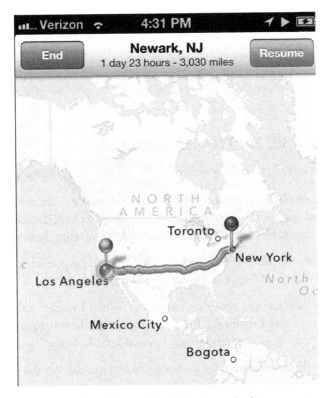

Almost Time to Road Trip. I can do this.

January 29, 2013 (Guadalupe, CA)

Fellow travelers!

Ugh! This is so not the week to not feel sparkly and shiny. Suck it up buttercup, it's going to be worth it. You're going home. I can do this. Send me love!

To finally heading home.

~Robin

*Although I barely knew the person I was about to share a life with and had never seen the space, it already felt as though I was going home. The entire experience felt familiar. It was as if it had been waiting for me all along.

January 30, 2013 (Guadalupe, CA)

Fellow travelers, Be gentle with each other. That's all.

To us.

~Robin

January 30, 2013 (Guadalupe, CA)

"Love brings up everything unlike itself." -Marianne Williamson

Fellow travelers! I haven't felt well the past few days. Let me keep it real: I was on the floor crying for my Mama a couple of days ago. I'm on the mend. However, I'm not quite back to traveling health.

I better handle that with a quickness because this gal gets back on the road in *two* days! Gracious be, send me love.

What I have learned about myself is this: When I neglect to tell the entire truth and I withhold, I feel it in my body. There is a part of me that screams until I acknowledge. I surrender, I hear you!

I'm unwilling to tolerate the pain any more. I'm ready for the ache in my head and my heart to quiet down.

And with that, it's confession time. Again.

I feel outta my mind scared. My chest is tight, my head is pounding and my blood pressure is up in the clouds. Hold please. Isn't this where I was when I started this journey? Gracious be, send more love.

Existing in that way is not an option. Tell the Truth, Robin.

The Truth is that I don't know what the purpose of this trip was and I'm ok with that. What I do know is that I'm not the same person I was at the start. The kiddo that first ventured out on the road was afraid of life, she ran from it. The woman that is starting on the second part of this journey embraces life, all of it. The hurt, the uncertain, the grief, the joy, the angst, the love...

The Truth is that even though I made it across this beautiful country once on kindness and faith, I'm uncertain that I can do it again.

The Truth is that I don't have any more answers than I did when I started and I'm ok with that as well. Life, for me, is not meant to be figured out. It just is. It is meant to be lived in joy, moment by moment.

The Truth is that I am ready to go home. I have connected with a gentle and sweet spirit that I want to nurture a relationship with. Home is where the love is. And in this moment, home is with them. I am ready to plant roots. I am ready to start a family. I am ready to share my heart. I'm all in, let's do this.

The Truth is that I am afraid to ask for anymore help even though that is what I am in need of.

The truth is that I could use a hug right about now.

And that, my friends, is Robin's Truth.

At the moment I'm in Santa Maria, California and I'm headed to Montclair, New Jersey very shortly. Total miles: 3,030. Currently, I am still in need of fuel for the trip. If what I have done has encouraged you, inspired your own journey or touched your heart, then please consider supporting me in any way you are willing to so that I can travel home. Any amount is welcomed and appreciated, it all helps.

And don't think that once I land in Jersey the Road Trip is over. Oh no, this trip ain't over until I send each and every one of you an invite to my very own housewarming party.

Thank you all for being my support system. Thank you for offering a hand to hold when I needed one. Thank you for having a listening ear during the late nights on the road. I could not have done this without you. That's the Truth.

Let's go home.

To the Road Trip!

~Robin

*In response to this post a fellow traveler wrote.

"I think you need to give yourself some credit, and when you can't do it for yourself it is best that someone do it for you. So I am gonna:

Top 10 lessons I have seen you learn along the way:
1. Some things aren't worth going back for.
2. Some things aren't worth crying over.
3. Some things are.
4. You are always exactly where you are supposed to be.
5. Running through cornfields is exactly as fun as you think it might be.
6. Taking the first step to mend a broken heart is more valuable than living in fear.
7. Taking leaps of faith means you have to have faith that the net will catch you.
8. People are incredible, they are loving, kind, supportive, and LIFE giving.
9. Everyday things are precious, a bed to sleep in, a hot meal, a loving hand, a helpful soul, clean clothes, warm clothes, a healthy body, a healthy car...
10. Counting your blessings instead of your losses is way more profitable."

Thank you for this, Joli. I needed that reminder.

January 31, 2013 (Guadalupe, CA)

I'm feeling all lovey today.

Fellow travelers! Everything I've experienced has brought me to this right now moment. I wouldn't change a thing. I'm so happy, and that's what this entire trip has been about for me.

Almost time to go home, friends.

To the Road Trip!

~Robin

February 1, 2013 (Guadalupe, CA)

"There is a power and a presence within us that can move any obstacle."
~A quote that a friend shared with me earlier from the book that she was reading. That was right on time.

Fellow travelers! Um, my plans aren't quite going as planned. And you know what? It's alright. It is! I was intending to have my car ready for the road but there are a few things (oil change, new tire) that I still want to get done. I'm going to spend the day taking care of that and then I'll get packed up. I also made the choice to attend one more Sunday at Agape. I'll visit their 6:30 am "early bird gets the word" service and then get on the road. Yes!

Since my travel plans changed and I wouldn't be heading back to Oregon, I had my friend ship the cards and gifts that you all sent shipped to me in California. I can not tell you the amount of childlike fun that I had with them last night! The toy VW bug in the picture is a present that my friend hand painted for me. Love it! Thanks again everyone, I'm grateful! Thank you cards from the road are on the way.

On a side note, I kinda flipped out last night. For real. It feels like a lot to handle right now and I had a moment. After a good night of rest, a cupcake and a reassuring talk, I'm now feeling as though I can do this. Again. This life deal is a moment by moment process for sure. That's the truth.

I have almost $300 of the $500 that it will take to get me from California to New Jersey. Although it doesn't appear that I have what I need, I still plan to get on the road with the same mantra that I had before: "All is well."

To the Road Trip!

~Robin

I love that I have the kind of friends that would hand paint a tiny VW bug for me. Thank you Aurora!

February 1, 2013 (Guadalupe, CA)

To my personal friends KiMani, Aurora, Victoria, Melissa, Jeanne as well as to all the page peoples, you all ROCK my world! Thank you for the Birthday love!

Best ever Road Trip birthday swag from the fellow travelers.

February 2, 2013 (Guadalupe, CA)

Dear Universe,

First, I love you! Second, I feel as if you don't believe that I want to go home. I know that obstacles are only real if I believe that they are. You taught me that. Howeva', the ones that you have currently placed on my path are appearing quite realish at the moment.

With that said: I, Robin Harris, state that it is my sincere and heartfelt intention to travel home with ease, grace and JOY! I affirm that all of my needs are provided for, always and in all ways. I am safe. I am loved. I am protected. My heart is filled with gratitude for the beautiful ways in which you show up in the people that I meet on this journey. Thank you! I open my heart to the experiences that you are about to share with me. I know that each person on this path is an opportunity for me to bless someone or to be blessed. Open my eyes to see it all. It's time to head home, please show me how. Thank you for having my back, I am grateful. Let's do this!

With thanks, love and an intact sense of humor,

~Robin

Fellow travelers, I found out last night that a friend passed away earlier in the week. After the initial shock and sadness in my heart lifted, I felt a sense of lightness for her. She loved to Salsa dance and her illness no longer allowed her to do that. In spite of her fading physical abilities, she continued to live each moment with everything that she had. A few months ago she started regularly changing her "current city" on Facebook to all the places she wanted to see but knew she would never have time to visit. This former powerhouse in the corporate world even changed her occupation to "works at McDonalds." I loved that woman. The way she lived, not her physical death, has made me want to embrace my life even more deeply. These are your moments, enjoy them. Please.

Stacey, I will miss you. You were my cheerleader even when I didn't know I needed one. I promise to randomly Salsa dance in store aisles as often as possible. To my friend Kimberly, I think of you every day. I love you both.

The Road Trip gets back on the road tomorrow. Good traveling vibes are appreciated.

To the Road Trip.

~Robin

I met Stacey virtually when I started my Choose Happiness page in 2011. She soon became my most vocal supporter and cheerleader. It wasn't until a year into our friendship that she shared she was battling ALS, a neurological disease that impacts the muscles and impairs physical function. In spite of that, she continued to encourage me in any way she could. We used to share quick pep talks on the phone and then when she lost her ability to speak, she would use her iPad to send me messages on Facebook. One day her message said that she was losing the use of her fingers and would no longer be able to connect.

I continued to send her messages with the hope that someone was reading them to her. I would always say to her that when I finished traveling, I was going to New Jersey to give her a hug. When I realized that where I would be moving to was 20 minutes from her, I was ecstatic! I headed to her page to send her a note and was stunned when I saw it filled with messages of condolences. My heart ached as I realized that I would never get the chance to hug my friend and thank her.

February 2, 2013 (Guadalupe, CA)

Fellow travelers, I am such a 12 year old at the moment. My 12 year old should not be in charge of anything ever.

I'm going with it.

To the Road Trip!

~Robin

February 3, 2013 (Guadalupe, CA. The morning I leave for New Jersey)

Fellow travelers, Wait a minute, wait a minute, wait a minute! I just remembered that this is supposed to be fun. Whew! That feels better. Regardless of what I do or don't have, I intend to enjoy every moment of this trip home!

Ok, back to packing. This puppy gets back on the road soon.

To the Road Trip!

~Robin

February 3, 2013 (Guadalupe, CA)

Fellow travelers, time to ride! Headed back to the East coast today. I can do this! I'm not quite convinced yet. I'm getting there, it's still early.

A quick check in before I get on the road to Los Angeles. I gotta tell you, I'm nervous at the moment. It's not about where I'm headed. It's more about the trip itself. It's as if I'm being asked to put everything that I have learned over the past months about faith, trust and fear into practice.

I gotta run so I can finish packing. One day I'm going to learn to pack the night before. That day is not today.

I'll check in tonight once I'm settled. Good traveling vibes and love are always appreciated!

Am I really doing this? Kiddo, it would appear that way. Let's do this!

Goodbye cabbage patch. Next stop, Los Angeles.

To the Road Trip!

~Robin

February 3, 2013 (West Hollywood, CA)

Fellow travelers! Safe and sound in a swanked out pad in West Hollywood that's all mine for the night thanks to one of you all from the page. You all are so kind to me, thank you Dora! The Universe has jokes. There were two people that I wanted to meet while in Los Angeles. I figured I missed my chance. I walked into Starbucks and there was one of them: Paolo from A Spoonful of Paolo! How about that? He was so handsome and sweet! Tomorrow, New Mexico. G'night friends.

Rest well everyone, I know I will.

To the Road Trip!

~Robin

A random meeting with Paolo from "A Spoonful of Paolo" at a Starbucks in Hollywood. Thank you Paolo for showing me what it looks like to dream BIG and then go live your dream.

February 4, 2013 (Los Angeles, CA)

Fellow travelers, temporary extended stay in Los Angeles, I'll tell you about it later.

On a side note, there ain't nothing like love.

To the Road Trip!

~Robin

February 5, 2013 (Los Angeles, CA)

Fellow travelers!

People care about me! At some point, I'm going to completely understand and honor that. Still in Los Angeles and overwhelmed with gratitude about it.

See what had happened was: I ended up staying in Los Angeles for longer than expected because I was in dire need of new tires. The family that was hosting me for the night (lovely folks from the Road Trip page) just happened to have 4 brand new tires on a car that they were getting ready to take to the junkyard. As I've said before, can't make this up. It took a few days to get the car towed and the tires switched, but it was worth the wait. I got to spend quality time with new friends and I had peace of mind for my travels ahead. Dora and family, I thank you for being another set of angels on my journey home.

To the Road Trip!

~Robin

February 6, 2013 (Los Angeles, CA)

Fellow travelers, Time to get back on the road!

Here's the thing: even though nothing has gone according to *my* plan, it's still perfect. It always is. I'm headed to Tucson or Mesa, AZ. If you know someone that can host me for a night, please let me know. I'll bring the tea.

I envision myself in a nice comfy space this evening where I will have a bit of quiet time to come chat here and update you. I'll check in tonight even if it's just to say "I'm here." I'm working on being a woman of my word. Some days I do better than others. Work in progress.

Thanks for all the love, it helps.

To the Road Trip!

-Robin

February 6, 2013 (Palm Desert, CA)

Fellow travelers, my most recent hosts taught me that everyone has a dream and a story. Often, all people need is someone to sit still long enough to listen to it. In Palm Desert, California and I have a few more hours of driving in me tonight. Will check in tomorrow.

Send good traveling vibes, love to you all.

To the Road Trip!

-Robin

February 7, 2013 (Las Cruces, NM)

Today is a "pants optional" kinda day on the Road Trip.

Good morning fellow travelers and New Mexico! It's amazing how far I can drive on motivation and a sugar high. I'm going to stay focused. I'll check my inbox when I stop again. If I can get through Texas tonight then that would be pure awesome sauce. There's a lotta tumbleweed out here, I'm just sayin'. We shall see.

Love you all and thanks for the encouragement.

Take a minute to go tell someone how much you appreciate them and why. It can make such a difference, more than you know.

To the Road Trip!

-Robin

Daybreak in Las Crucas, New Mexico

February 7, 2013 (Van Horn, TX)

Fellow travelers,

I'm in Texas, yes ma'am! That's all I've got at the moment. It was a long day, peoples. I'm out. See you tomorrow. Go love up on someone, just 'cause.

To Texas!

~Robin

I was running on pure adrenaline, love and coffee at this point.

February 8, 2013 (Balch Springs, TX)

Fellow travelers!

This morning I woke up and had no idea what state I was in. Turns out it's Texas. Still. Good to know. Didn't get a lot of driving done last night as my body needed to rest. However, now I'm refreshed and ready! Apparently there is a little fella named (Winter storm) Nemo headed towards New Jersey. Huh. And you know what? I am *still* looking forward to being there more than I can say. I'm headed home!

I had a really beautiful morning, hope you did as well. Do something that brings you joy today. You deserve it.

To the Road Trip!

~Robin

February 9, 2013 (Little Rock, AR)

Fellow travelers!

In Arkansas, all is well. Wifi hasn't been great out here. Feeling a bit worn down and ready to get to Jersey. 1000 more miles to go. The day started out lovely as I had the chance to spend time with one of you all. I always enjoy that! Thank you, Larry. You are as kind as I knew you would be.

After our chat, I got on the road and was feeling groovy! Then traffic stopped. For 5 hours. Aye, dios mio. I'm a fairly patient person. With that said, my nerves are a bit worn thin at the moment. I'm tired. I even changed my route to one that was shorter. I will miss visiting a few friends but I'll plan a trip out this summer. The kiddo will be back

To the Road Trip!

~Robin

My "I've been in the same spot for 5 hours" face.

February 9, 2013 (Gordonsville, TN)

Sweet peas and rice, 13 more hours to go.

Fellow travelers, I have had the same conversation with three different people in the past week. Each time I shared that I have been on the road for 9 months, each one said: it's almost like a rebirth, you were born again on this trip.

Indeed I was.

To the Road Trip!

~Robin

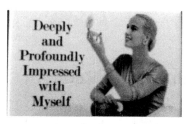

A perfectly timed magnet that I saw along the way. After 2,000 miles, I could honestly and without hesitation say that I was quite impressed with myself.

February 9, 2013 (even later that day in Memphis, TN)

Fellow travelers, life is too short to wait.

In Memphis, 900 miles to go!

To the Road Trip!

~Robin

February 9, 2013 (seriously late in Tennessee City, TN)

Fellow travelers, almost to Nashville! 700 miles to go...

I'm not the same person I was 9 months ago. My heart is open. I am living fully and in the moment. For that, I am so grateful.

I'm not sure where I am but I'm getting closer. Thanks for the love, everyone.

To the Road Trip!

~Robin

February 9, 2013 (the never ending day in Crossville, TN)

Fellow travelers! My mechanic said my car Zora wouldn't last the 3000 mile trip home. Ha! My check engine light came on literally 2 miles after I started out on Monday yet she is still holding her own. Double ha! I am currently out of funds for gas and I am 600 miles away from my New Jersey destination. Ok, that one isn't quite as hilarious.

What I do know is that tomorrow, I will be home. What I am unclear on is how that will happen. Universe, I hand it over to you as I have done many times before. I trust you.

If this journey has inspired you, encouraged you or touched your heart in any way, then please consider sharing a bit of support for the last few miles of Robin's Road Trip to Freedom.

There is a home cooked meal, a warm bed and a loving heart waiting for me. I'm ready to head home.

Thank you for your kindness, everyone. I could not have done this without you.

To one of the last few times I'll be saying this, to the Road Trip!

~Robin

A picture of me during the journey home. Now that's a happy woman.

I was so close. I had one last need and I reached out with the most open heart that I had ever had. Seconds after I posted this, my email notifications started going off letting me know that I had received a donation. They poured in one after another. Along with the gifts came notes and messages from people who, although they had followed the entire journey, had never commented, donated or shared in the trip in any way. They wanted to thank me for inspiring them and reminding them to go and live. I was in awe. I was overwhelmingly grateful in a way that I did not have words for. After a few moments of giving thanks and letting go of tears, I filled up my tank and headed back on the road.

February 9, 2013 (Farragut, TN)

Wow, fellow travelers. Thank you! I love you all. I want to get back on the road but I'll write you each tomorrow. Your kindness overwhelms me. Blessings to you all.

Let's go home.

~Robin

February 10, 2013 (West Orange, NJ) 3:30pm

Fellow travelers, I'm almost there. It doesn't feel quite real…

What a Journey.

~Robin

As I neared the final two hours, exhaustion set in. It took everything in me to stay alert. I turned the radio all the way up and rolled the windows down. I silently prayed that my off key singing and the frigid temperature would keep me awake. When the GPS displayed that I was ten minutes away from my destination, I pulled into the first parking lot I saw. As fate would have it, it was a Whole Foods parking lot. I made an effort to freshen up and calm my nerves. However, after four days on road, there was not much that could be done for either one. I stopped for a moment of quiet, took a breath and returned to the final few miles of road home.

February 10, 2013 (Montclair, NJ) 4pm

Fellow travelers, Finally made it to New Jersey! It turned out to be a longer trip than expected, however, it was good. Ready for a nap, a meal and a shower. Thank you all for the help in getting here, it wouldn't have been possible without you all. Glad to be home! I'll check in tomorrow, love to you all.

I'm home.

To the end of the Road Trip!

~Robin

As I came to my last turn towards a new journey, my heart raced with anticipation. As I pulled into the parking lot, I glanced at the doorway and saw my love there waiting for me. It was the happiest moment of my life.

After 9 months on Robin's Road Trip to Freedom, I was home.

The final stretch of highway on my Road Trip journey.

February 25, 2013 (Montclair, NJ)

Fellow homebodies! I'm not sure that has the ring I'm going for, I'm open for suggestions. And yes, I totally deserve the side eye. I have no excuse as to why I evaporated for the past couple of weeks. All I can say is that the kiddo needed rest and a social media reprieve. That's the truth, Ruth. And it wasn't only rest from the trip; it was rest from the past few years. Those of you that have been with me a while know that this journey has been more extended than just the Road Trip. It's been a lengthy path to get to this point.

To start: a heaping THANK YOU to all of you that supported me in any way in going home. It was because of your generous donations, kind well wishes and good traveling vibes that I was able to travel from California to New Jersey with a quickness, safely and with ease. I send gratitude to you all, from my heart to yours. Thank you again.

Let's get caught up…

Where are you? New Jersey, baby!
Are you ok? I'm well. I'm really well. Thanks for checking in.
Wait, why are you in New Jersey? I'm here because I fell in love.

Hold the phone, buttercup. Do you mean to tell me that you drove across the country (one mo' time) to explore a relationship and *live* with someone that you had been talking to on the phone for a month? What?! I get the feeling that you Mamas out there want to give me a loving and concerned shake to get some sense in my head. That's fair. Were my Mom still here, I'm sure she would thank you for it.

Howevs, here's the deal: This entire journey has been about following my heart, why would this venture be any different? I could choose to put limits on what "following my heart" looks like. For instance, I could only listen to it when I was certain that it was going to unfold the way I wanted it to. Or, I could only pay attention to the whispers when I was sure that it wouldn't cause me hurt, upset or disappointment. Sweet baby billy goats, where is the fun in that? Over the past nine months I have made the commitment to embrace life: *all* of it. In this moment, that includes embracing the uncertainty of it as well.

I came to this new experience with an open heart, a willing spirit and a gentle anticipation that did not demand anything. As a result, I have found the person that I am going to walk down the aisle with one day. I have found the person that I plan to raise little travelers with. I have found the person that loves my Road Trippin' behind, quirks, scars and all.

One more thing: The person that I love and that loves me is a woman. I'd like to introduce you to KiMani. She has my heart.

I questioned if I wanted to share that with you all. I wondered if it even mattered. I now realize that it doesn't…which is why I shared it. I know, that makes no kinda sense. In short, it is what it is. And what it is, is love. Should that happen to insult every single solitary fiber of your personal being, then that's ok. It's still love.

I'm happy. I'm loved. I'm nurtured. I'm appreciated. My heart is full. I feel alive. I'm grateful!

Those are the pieces that matter. All the rest, nah man.

As I bring this catch-up post to a close, I want to share this: I don't have any answers. I don't always do things "right." And I'm not unique in my story. What I am is a person that wants my remaining time on this planet to be fulfilling and joyful. To do that, I stopped requiring that life make sense. I pried fear's grip from my throat and began to breathe again, I made a leap of faith on behalf of my own life and I always, always, always continued to move forward. That's all folks. I made a different choice. You can as well, at any moment.

I can't even begin to imagine what is ahead. I sit in gratitude for what is, what has been and what is to come.

Friends, I'm home!

With Love,

~Robin

This was taken a few hours after I arrived home. Do you see the look on my face? That's deliriousness and complete happiness all in one. I had slept maybe ten hours in four days. In spite of that, I still wanted to head out on the town and spend time with her as soon as I got there. It took a minute to convince her that it was a rational idea, she was concerned. As for me, I wasn't thinking about sleep. I only wanted to wrap myself up in as much love as I could in that moment. And that's what I did.

*As I wrote in an earlier afterthought, the person that I fell in love with was a woman. However, this post was my first time sharing that with the fellow travelers. A handful of them privately messaged me after the fact. Many of them gently shared that they already knew and thanked me for my honesty. My attempts to be subtle had given me away early on. The amount of support and love that I received from the fellow travelers was true to form for them.

EPILOGUE

It has now been nearly three years since I ended Robin's Road Trip to Freedom. I found that putting my experience down on paper was more challenging than I expected. The Road Trip was the hardest thing I have ever done in my life. Revisiting it in countless edits and rewrites was incredibly painful at times. And yet, with persistent dedication (involving countless dramatic tantrums) and continual encouragement from KiMani, I have completed it. For that, I am humbled and grateful.

Life has continued to expand and open up in beautiful ways over the past two years. To start, KiMani and I were engaged a few months later in 2013 and we were married on September 14, 2014. In less than a month we will celebrate our 1 year anniversary. If the entire Road Trip journey was needed to get me to this point in my life, then it was completely worth it. I wouldn't change anything. I love my life, I adore my wife and I give thanks for the relationship that we are nurturing together. On a side note, remember the never ending Spiritual Life Development program that I couldn't seem to pry myself away from? Looking back, I now believe that I was there waiting for our paths to cross. Once we connected, I found myself feeling complete with the program.

I am currently sitting on an airplane writing the last few words of my story. I am also accompanying my wife on her final trip as a Flight Attendant. Once we land, she will be officially retired from 26 years at the Airline. She is completing this part of her journey so that she can fully step into the next one. KiMani has committed herself to the Healing Center that she founded 2 years ago, Women Healing Zone. She is walking in Faith to pursue what she loves and to share her light with the world. I am honored to support her on her path. I am a proud wife.

This right now moment feels incredibly full circle to me. We are both completing a cycle; I am thankfully completing this book and she is taking her last flight. In the morning I begin sharing my writing with others and she opens the doors to Women Healing Zone full time.

As for the future, I like the quote that Abraham Hicks said: "Be deeply satisfied and ready for more."

That's about where I am right now.

-Robin

Our Wedding Day: September 14th, 2014

ACKNOWLEDGEMENTS AND GRATITUDE

I will always believe that there is good in the world. I would not be where I am if not for your kindness.

*

In acknowledgement of Pamela, Joli, Victoria, Jenn, Aurora, Brad and Rachel, thank you. It was your gifts of creativity, willingness and patience that supported me in completing this.

For every gallon of gas, each home cooked meal, all the prayers for safe travels, every encouraging word and the continued love and support, I send gratitude to:

LaKeisha, Amy C.M., Mrs. Campbell, Erika, Marie, Gayle, Edith, Sharon H., Ivan and family, Jamie, Amy M.S. and family, Christian, Cathy, Glenn, Roselle Family, Michael, Lori C., Ingrid, Lori-Ann, Alan, Jason, Kimberly, Lori Y., Jeanne, Shari, Teena, Kirby, Aimee, Randall, Kathleen, Jane, Jo, Lynn, Maq, Georgianne, Mia, Sharon B., Omayra, Rev.Nancy, Kimberly, Jon, Laura, Stacy, Jennifer and family, Dennis, Doreen, Liz, Kelly S., Karen, Lorna, Robin LJ and family, Ellen, Ingrid H., Rev. Leandrah, Coach Ade, Chey, Carolyn, Linda, Cindy, Shannon, Michele, Carlie, Kris, Barbara, Sharon H., Nicole, Tammy, Mary, Diane, Anthony, Carmen and family, David, Carline, Anette, Kenna, Elizabeth, Ola, Ingrid, Karen, Shani, Kris, Monica, Paula, Gina, Alison, Sharolyn, Margaret, Kelly S. Shawn, Rachel G., Barnaby, Christian, P.J., Angie, Jason, Karen B., Tracie, Jen, Chad, Keith, Amy K., Cheryl, Sheila, Michel, Hannamari, Ron, Phillip, North, Nadja, Geske, Anthony, Jeffrey, Michele, Janet, Sarita Denise, Kea, Crystal, Jenna, Jared, Wendi, Rhonda, Erika, Lynn, Kelly M., Damon, Stacey, Kate, Colleen, Nat, Tessica, Jen, Shaddai, Janey, Marie, Shelby, Ivete, Sue-Ann, L.A., Cindy, Kimberly, MacKenzie, Patty, Rose Mary, Kelly, Larry, David, Debra, Linda, Kat, Brian, The Agape Family, Dora, Jayde, Donna, Fran, Kim, the Chapman family and most of all to my love, KiMani.

Thank you, I will pay it forward.
To the Road Trip!
-Robin

*And remember that post where I wrote everything that I desired in a home? I received everything I wrote and so much more. There's plenty of almond milk and Coconut Bliss Ice cream for when you come visit.

The doormat to my new home when I arrived. It read: Home is where Happy lives.

Indeed it is.

*

To Visions Manifested.

Made in the USA
Middletown, DE
07 September 2023

38112588R00129